D0325353

The Church Is Our Mother

• • •

Seven Ways She Inspires Us to Love

• • •

GINA LOEHR

servant

AN IMPRINT OF
FRANCISCAN MEDIA
Cincinnati, Ohio

Cover and book design by Mark Sullivan
Cover image © istock | Tamara Kulikova

LIBRARY OF CONGRESS CATALOGING-IN-PUBLICATION DATA
Names: Loehr, Gina, author.
Title: The church is our mother : seven ways she inspires us to love / Gina Loehr.
Description: Cincinnati : Servant, 2016. | Includes bibliographical references.
Identifiers: LCCN 2016018612 | ISBN 9781632530202 (trade paper)
Subjects: LCSH: Church. | Catholic Church—Doctrines. | Motherhood—Religious
aspects—Catholic Church. | Mothers—Religious life.
Classification: LCC BX1746 .L62125 2016 | DDC 262/.7—dc23
LC record available at https://lccn.loc.gov/2016018612

Published by Servant
an imprint of Franciscan Media
28 W. Liberty St.
Cincinnati, OH 45202
www.FranciscanMedia.org

Printed in the United States of America.
Printed on acid-free paper.
16 17 18 19 20   5 4 3 2 1

FOR MY CHILDREN
Your names are written on my heart
(and hidden in this book!)

Contents

Introduction

"The Church is woman, she is mother, and this is beautiful. You must consider and go deeper into this."[1]

When Pope Francis spoke these words to me and my companions during a private audience at the Vatican, I felt a personal tug on my heart, a kind of commission. We were commemorating the twenty-fifth anniversary of Pope St. John Paul II's apostolic letter *Mulieris Dignitatem* (On the Dignity and Vocation of Women), a document that had profoundly touched my life by changing my understanding of women and the Church.

This letter brought me back to the Catholic faith when I had read it for the first time some fifteen years earlier. Its beautiful vision of the value of "the feminine 'genius'" in the Church and the world, along with its recognition of the significance of motherhood, captivated me.[2] I had sworn off motherhood, not surprisingly, at the same time that I had sworn off Mother Church. But *Mulieris Dignitatem* helped me to return to the embrace of my mother, the Church, and personally to embrace my vocation to marriage and motherhood as well.

Now, a decade and a half after first encountering this document, I found myself sitting in the magnificent Clementine Hall with the Holy Father himself (while bouncing my fourth baby on my lap) as he called for further reflection upon these life-changing themes.

Yes, I agreed with Pope Francis. I should think more deeply about this. Why do we refer to the Church as "she"? Why is *she* affectionately called "Mother Church"? What does this reveal about the nature of the Church and about the nature of motherhood?

These questions are intertwined. Thinking about motherhood can help us understand the Church, and thinking about the Church can help us understand motherhood. In this book, I will draw from my experience as a mother of six children (and as a daughter and granddaughter!) to reflect upon the rich meaning of this traditional title.

In the chapters that follow, I will examine seven ways in which Mother Church, like any mother, shows her love for us as she creates, cares, teaches, accepts, sacrifices, heals, and celebrates. The final chapter of the book will turn to the Blessed Mother, considering seven special titles of Mary and how the spirituality behind them can enlighten and strengthen mothers in particular. Throughout the book, I have also incorporated reflections from other mothers whose insights and experiences will contribute to our understanding of these ideas.

A study guide at the back of the book offers the opportunity to reflect more deeply upon the themes of the main chapters. In this study I will invite mothers to explore with me what we can learn about our maternal vocation from specific elements of the life of the Church, including the liturgy, the *Catechism*, the lives of the saints, and the sacraments. Eight study sections correspond to each of the eight chapters of the book. This study guide can easily be incorporated into a group setting, such as a mothers' book club or fellowship group, but it is also well suited for individual use.

I hope that encountering the content of this book may be a contribution to the task that the Holy Father has laid before us. In fact, Pope Francis has already offered a few initial reflections to get us started. In one Wednesday general audience he commented, "For me it is one of the most beautiful images of the Church: Mother Church! In what sense and in what way is the Church mother? We start with the human reality of motherhood: what makes a mother?"[3] We will explore these questions throughout the pages that follow.

Although the book is addressed primarily to mothers, others are most welcome to explore these themes with us—men included! *Spiritual* mothers especially—whether consecrated or lay women, and particularly women who are mothering children with whom they share no biological connection—should consider themselves an important part of these reflections. As Pope St. John Paul II wrote in *Mulieris Dignitatem*, "motherhood '*according to the Spirit*'"[4] is expressed even by women who have not borne children when they serve those in need, care for children and the elderly, teach, give medical care, or show their concern for others through any number of professions, ministries, and vocations. Thus spiritual motherhood is, in fact, intimately connected to the mission of Mother Church.

So let us begin our reflections upon how *the Church is our mother*, bearing in mind that this book will only scratch the surface. Ultimately, I hope that the material presented here will serve as a springboard for others to delve ever more deeply into the beautiful mystery of Mother Church, and to reflect upon the tremendous importance of the vocation of motherhood itself.

CHAPTER ONE ··· Mothers Create

I wept the whole ride home. My husband, Joe, was driving me and our brand new baby girl back from the hospital. She was bundled up in her baby bucket in the backseat, sleeping peacefully, and I was sobbing like an infant up front. Joe didn't try to figure me out or encourage me to be quiet. He just put his hand on mine and let me cry.

My emotions were all over the place. The gravity of the situation had hit me like a psychological avalanche. We were really parents now. We had brought this person into the world, and suddenly we were responsible for her! Leaving the nurses and doctors behind, we were setting off to our own home to chart our own course.

I was petrified.

At the same time, I was exuberant. Our baby was healthy and beautiful, and I loved her already. She hadn't done anything to earn this love, yet to me she was of infinite value. The gratitude for her existence, the desire to protect and provide for her, the hopes and dreams that were already swirling in my head, were all filling my heart to overflowing.

And, of course, I was hormonal and exhausted. After twenty-four hours of labor that marched straight into the round-the-clock nursing routine, I was sleep deprived; and my body was recovering from the effects of childbirth. My physical resources were depleted and I was shaky and weak as I embarked on the most important task of my entire life.

All of this was collectively absorbing my consciousness at once. It was a bit too much to handle. For me, anyway. Joe told me later that he was just thinking about oncoming traffic during that ride home. Now a dad, his primary concern was not getting into a car accident. So simple, so appropriate. Such a good balance to basket-case me. And, I believe, such an illustration of the fact that, although we are both equally parents, motherhood is not the same as fatherhood.

Bringing this baby into the world required so much of me, so much of my personhood was involved—physical, spiritual, and emotional. As John Paul II wrote in *Mulieris Dignitatem*:

> *The woman's motherhood constitutes a special 'part' in this shared parenthood*, and the most demanding part. Parenthood—even though it belongs to both—is realized much more fully in the woman, especially in the pre-natal period. It is the woman who "pays" directly for this shared generation, which literally absorbs the energies of her body and soul. It is therefore necessary that *the man* be fully aware that in their shared parenthood he owes *a special debt to the woman*.[5]

Yes, my energies were completely absorbed by this experience of becoming a mother. Though I have gone through childbirth multiple times since then, none of the other trips home were nearly so dramatic. For with this particular transition, I encountered the reality of becoming a mother: instead of not having a child, I now had one.

For the *first* time, I was a mom.

The awareness of what had just taken place was brand new and utterly astonishing. Intellectually, I had of course known that a person had been developing inside my body during pregnancy— there were ultrasound images and sensations of kicks and somersaults along with the obvious expansion of my waistline. None of this, however, quite prepared me for the shock of actually meeting that person face-to-face. Holding her little curled-up self, nursing her, and watching her wiggle were absolutely captivating. I couldn't believe that this perfect little human being had been living inside of me for nine months. It was so surreal to think that I had something to do with *creating* her.

I recall a few days after our return home when I was sitting in the walk-in closet at 2:00 AM (where I could turn on the light without disturbing Joe). After I finished nursing, I held my newborn baby upright at my face level and just gazed into her little eyes for several minutes. Again, I began to weep. I was so moved by her presence, her beauty, her innocence. I felt this tremendous connection to her, even though we had just "met" and we couldn't exchange a word. I knew she was my child, that I was her mother, and that we had indeed been together, establishing a silent bond, since the first moment of her existence within me.

During those first months there were so many moments like this. There were so many times when I simply stared at her and marveled at her being. I felt as if I could just sit and watch her for hours on end. Look at her blink! See her tiny hand wave around! She just yawned! Watch her breathe! It was all so marvelous, beholding this person, the fruit of my womb.

It's clear to me that motherhood is a kind of miracle. Without a doubt, God is behind the whole thing, and the creation of these new people is not just a matter of my initiative or my nurturing. I am a *co*-creator in *pro*creation. But even though I partner with God and my husband in this process, the fact remains that, as a mother, I participate in an utterly unique way in bringing my children into existence. It is through my body, my energy, my physical resources, that these human beings are built.

When I am sick and depleted during the early weeks of my pregnancies, I can often muster only enough energy to pass time reading in the recliner. Sometimes even reading is too much and I just... sit. During these long, difficult months, when there is so much I "should" be doing, so many tasks going undone, so many projects that simply have to wait, I have learned to reassure myself. It may look as if I'm not doing a blessed thing, but I am in fact being extremely productive: I am building a person from scratch. My body is churning away, creating fingernails and eyelids and organs and nerves and all the rest. I eat and drink and breathe, and a new little Loehr grows and grows and grows.

Mulieris Dignitatem reflects on this remarkable cooperation with the Creator:

> According to the Bible, the conception and birth of a new human being are accompanied by the following words of the woman: "*I have brought a man into being with the help of the Lord*" (Gen 4:1). This exclamation of Eve, the "mother of all the living" is repeated every time a new human being comes into the world. It expresses the woman's joy and awareness that she is sharing in the great mystery of eternal generation.... Motherhood involves a special communion with the mystery of life, as it develops in the woman's womb.[6]

"A special communion with the mystery of life"—this sharing in the creation of new physical life is inherently connected to the very nature of human motherhood. And because the Church is inherently connected to the creation of new *spiritual* life, she too is a mother.

Mother Church Creates

In his encyclical letter *Mater et Magistra* (Mother and Teacher), Pope St. John XXIII referred to the Church as the mother and teacher of all nations. He explained it in this way: "To her was entrusted by her holy Founder the twofold task of giving life to her children and of teaching them and guiding them—both as individuals and as nations—with maternal care."[7]

This image of the Church as a life-giving mother is nothing new. It's really a standard part of the Catholic landscape. The concept of "Mother Church" is ever present, but it has a tendency to blend in with the background. Those of us who have been Catholic for a while may just glaze over this traditional title when we hear it in passing. After all, it's been floating around since the earliest days of Christianity. But in order to give the concept its due respect, the history and depth of the term *Ecclesia Mater* (Mother Church) is worth a bit of our deliberate attention.

When I first began researching all of this, I searched for passages where the title appears in Church documents. It turns out that the title shows up all over the place. But for all of its frequency, I did not find much explanation or detail about the meaning or history of this name "Mother Church." Most often, it was used almost as a nickname to identify the Church, but in connection to some other theological theme or discussion.

So I began to ponder whether the title was more sentimental and affectionate than theologically substantial—an analogy but little else. *Perhaps it's just a nice feeling to think of the Church as mother*, I thought. *Is that all there is to it?* I wondered. It didn't take long to resolve that question.

Upon opening a book entitled *The Motherhood of the Church* by the great twentieth century Jesuit theologian, Henri de Lubac, I found the answer in the first sentence. "When a Christian who knows what he is saying speaks of the Church as his mother, he is not giving way to some sentimental impulse; he is expressing a reality."[8] So, I read on, in the hopes of becoming a Christian who knows what she is saying!

Throughout the pages of his book, Father de Lubac emphasizes that having the Church as our mother is neither a novel concept nor an obscure ideology. Rather, this ecclesial maternity is inscribed in the very nature of the Church, and our participation in her life truly makes us her children. But this claim does not belong to de Lubac alone. Someone much more influential got this ball rolling about two thousand years ago.

Jesus himself used specifically maternal imagery when he exclaimed, "Jerusalem, Jerusalem, the city that kills the prophets and stones those who are sent to it! How often have I desired to gather your children together as a hen gathers her brood under her wings, and you were not willing!" (Matthew 23:37; Luke 13:34). St. Augustine interpreted this mother hen to be the Church that Jesus commissioned to carry on the motherly task he began on earth.[9]

But still centuries before Augustine, great Christian writers and saints saw the connection between the Church and motherhood. In his Letter to the Galatians, St. Paul described his ecclesial work in motherly terms, saying, "My little children, for whom I am again in the pain of childbirth until Christ is formed in you" (Gal 4:19). As Pope St. John Paul II explained, "In order to illustrate the Church's fundamental mission, [Paul] finds nothing better than the reference to motherhood."[10]

Also, in letters to the Ephesians and to the Corinthians, Paul explains how the Church is the bride of Christ. This paved the way for understanding the holy bride, the Church, as our mother. As the *Catechism of the Catholic Church* puts it, "The Church is the Bride of Christ: he loved her and handed himself over for her. He has purified her by his blood and made her the fruitful mother of all God's children" (*CCC*, 808).

Building upon these scriptural references, as early as the second century, saints and theologians were using the title *Ecclesia Mater*.[11] The Fathers of the Church incorporated the idea into their theological treatises and letters. Especially influential among them in regard to understanding Mother Church was St. Cyprian, Bishop of Carthage, who was martyred in AD 258.

In at least thirty different sources, this African saint spoke of the *Ecclesia Mater* in order to inspire, encourage, and instruct the faithful. To those who were imprisoned for their faith during the Decian persecutions, he wrote that Mother Church was glorified and her tears were wiped dry by their courage.[12] In his treatise *On the Unity of the Church*, he emphasized that there is only one head (Christ) and one mother (the Church) and that "by her bearing we are born, by her milk we are nourished, by her breath do we live."[13]

St. Cyprian's most famous formulation on the subject came from the same treatise and has earned a place in the *Catechism of the Catholic Church*. "The Church is the mother of all believers," the *Catechism* states, going on to quote Cyprian: "'No one can have God as Father who does not have the Church as Mother'" (CCC, 181).

Other figures in this era—including St. Irenaeus, Tertullian, St. Clement of Alexandria, and Origen—also spoke of the Church as mother and understood that the idea was more than a metaphor. Together the instructions of these ancient Fathers clarified that this title "signifies life as we are born from her womb; it signifies identity as we are offspring of the bride of Christ; it signifies nourishment as from her hands we receive food and drink, the very body and blood of our Lord Jesus Christ."[14]

Confirming these concepts, the nineteenth-century German theologian Matthias Scheeben wrote, "The motherhood of the church is not an empty title.... This motherhood is as real as the presence of Christ is real in the Eucharist, or as real as the supernatural life that exists in the children of God."[15]

So, "Mother Church" isn't just a fluffy nickname or a sentimental strategy that helps people submit to ecclesial authority. The Church's motherhood is a spiritual reality that profoundly affects the lives of believers. In fact, the famous convert to Catholicism Cardinal John Henry Newman once said that it was through his reading and encounter with the Church of the Fathers that "I found my spiritual Mother."[16]

The more I thought about all this, the more I came to realize that the Church really is *my* mother, too. She isn't a vague maternal force for a generic collection of anonymous people. This Mother truly nurtures *us*—each one of us. And for those of us who are baptized Christians, the Church has actually given birth to us on a spiritual level.

Indeed, it's through baptism in particular that we become God's children. In a Wednesday general audience on the topic of Mother Church, Pope Francis said, "The Church gives us the life of faith in Baptism: that is the moment in which she gives birth to us as children of God, the moment she gives us the life of God, she engenders us as a mother would."[17] John's Gospel explains, "But to all who received him, who believed in his name, he gave power to become children of God, who were born, not of blood nor of the will of the flesh nor of the will of man, but of God" (John 1:12–13). Being born of God is often referred to as being born again or born anew. In his exchange with Nicodemus, Jesus speaks of this reality. Acknowledging the difference between physical and spiritual birth, he nonetheless insists that there is the possibility for a true birth on the spiritual level:

> Now there was a Pharisee named Nicodemus, a leader of the Jews. He came to Jesus by night and said to him, "Rabbi, we know that you are a teacher who has come from God; for no one can do these signs that you do apart from the presence of God." Jesus answered him, "Very truly, I tell you, no one can see the kingdom of God without being born from above." Nicodemus said to him, "How can anyone be born after having grown old? Can one enter a second time into the mother's womb and be born?" Jesus answered, "Very truly, I tell you, no one can enter the kingdom of God without being born of water and Spirit. What is born of the flesh is flesh, and what is born of the Spirit is spirit. Do not be astonished that I said to you, 'You must be born from above.'" (John 3:1–7)

The reference to "being born of water and Spirit" is of course baptism, in which we are washed with water and filled with the Holy Spirit. In this great sacrament of initiation, the Church creates new Christians and welcomes them lovingly into her arms. Ever since Pentecost, when Peter and the other apostles baptized thousands of people, the Church has been responsible for celebrating baptism.[18] The children of God are thus born of this spiritual Mother, and initiated into the family of God.

The *Catechism* teaches that baptism is foundational to Christian life and serves as "the gateway to life in the Spirit" (CCC, 1213). Through this baptismal "gate" we are able to enter into the other sacraments of the Church and receive the graces they offer us. In addition, baptism frees us from sin and enables us to be "reborn as sons of God" (CCC, 1213). It also incorporates us into the Church and joins us to her mission.[19]

Although God can work outside the bounds of sacramental baptism, we know that through this sacred rite men and women are welcomed into a special communion with God and with other believers. Just as my children become members of my family when I bring them into the world, so too our baptism incorporates us into the family of the Church. This supernatural membership prevents us from being orphans who have to fend for themselves in the spiritual wilderness. Once born, we are not forgotten. "Blessed be the God and Father of our Lord Jesus Christ!" St. Peter exclaims in his first letter. "By his great mercy he has given us a new birth into a living hope" (1 Peter 1:3).

The Old Testament prophet Isaiah revealed God's maternal concern for his children: "Can a woman forget her nursing child, or show no compassion for the child of her womb? Even these may forget, yet I will not forget you" (Isaiah 49:15). The Church is like God's partner through whom this compassion is put into practice. The bride of Christ—his "helpmate," the Church—takes something spiritual like God's compassion and makes it concrete and tangible.

So it is that the spiritual reality of new birth for our souls, at the hands of Mother Church, feels refreshing like water, smells sweet like chrism, and shines brightly like the flame of the baptismal candle. In the embrace of Mother Church, the neophyte hears words of welcome and feels the touch of another human hand. These gestures and physical elements are some of the gifts that we receive from the Church. Instead of floating unsecured in an abyss of abstract religious ideas, our faith gives us the comforting touch of a mother.

But this touch is not just symbolic. When we are touched by the Church—especially through the ministry of her priests in the sacraments—we are truly changed. The encounter is effective spiritually, not just physically. All of the sacraments give us a kind of rebirth that creates our souls anew. Throughout our lives we are renewed and reinvigorated by our encounter with Christ in his Church. The *Catechism* describes this lifelong process:

> The seven sacraments touch all the stages and all the important moments of Christian life: they give birth and increase, healing and mission to the Christian's life of faith. There is thus a certain resemblance between the stages of natural life and the stages of the spiritual life. (CCC, 1210)

A mother journeys with her children all the way through their lives. She does not abandon her maternal mission when they are grown, though that mission certainly takes on different characteristics. The Church, too, accompanies us every step of the way. While baptism gives us birth into the Church, the other sacraments in their own way also nurture our souls as needed.

Together with baptism, the other sacraments of initiation are Eucharist and confirmation. This trifecta makes us full members of the Church, like older children who can thoughtfully participate in all the elements of family life. But more than just milestones of belonging, these sacraments change our souls.

When we receive confirmation, the graces of baptism come to full fruition as we are filled with the gifts of the Holy Spirit. Our souls are sealed with an "indelible spiritual mark" (CCC, 1304) as our membership in the Church itself is confirmed. "By the sacrament of Confirmation," the Catechism tells us, the baptized "are more perfectly bound to the Church and are enriched with a special strength of the Holy Spirit" (CCC, 1285).

When we receive the Eucharist, we accept our Mother's invitation to share in a kind of family banquet. But it is more than a communal meal. In the Eucharist we truly receive Jesus's Body and Blood into our bodies, and along with that we receive healing and strength for our souls.

The sacraments of healing, which are the sacraments of reconciliation and anointing of the sick, also in their own way nurture our souls and bodies. And the sacraments of vocation—matrimony and holy orders—offer those called to them the continual daily assistance of actual grace.

We don't do anything to earn all of this. A mother's love for her children is not conditional. The Church offers the sacraments of initiation and healing to anyone who sincerely wants to receive them. We have access to this new life simply by asking for it. It's important to note, however, that the maternal concern of the Church is not only for those who ask for baptism. I care for my family in a particular way, but that doesn't mean that I don't care about anyone else. The Church also includes in her mission all people, whether or not they are believers.

Of course the Church hopes to bless all people through baptism, but the unbaptized are still under the care of Mother Church. She wants what is best for all of humanity, for every man, woman, and child brought into physical existence through the power of God. This is why the Church seeks not only to protect spiritual life through her efforts of evangelization and baptism, but also to protect physical life. She defends the dignity of every human person by advocating for the right to life and fighting against any ideologies or programs that would threaten that right.

Mother Church is eager to bear new children, to love them and nurture them throughout their lives, and to protect their God-given dignity. Because Christ died and rose to assure our salvation, his bride, the Church, wants nothing more than to take full advantage of what the Bridegroom won for us. She wants to lavish graces upon us, to welcome us into her embrace, and to see us flourish in every possible way.

Another Mother's Voice: Rachel's Story

Rachel is the mother of two young daughters.

Last Sunday I went to Communion with a little secret: As I approached the Communion rail to receive the Body and Blood of our Lord, my six-week-old infant was actually in the act of nursing under my wrap. As I knelt there, I found myself thinking of how my baby could receive Communion with me at that moment through a kind of spiritual osmosis passing from my body to her own.

It made me feel extremely feminine and mysterious, in a Mona Lisa sort of way, and I wondered if Mary of Nazareth had any other interesting maternal secrets that she pondered in her heart besides the ones St. Luke knew about.

Maybe she marveled at her baby's wondrous first awareness of the world around him (a marvel that has caused me wonder, too), a world that she secretly knew he had come to save. Maybe she pondered his little face, looking for features that might be from her side of the family, in awe of any that seemed to come from his Father's side!

Maybe she suspected, as I have, that no one else would be as enthralled with the miraculous shape of her child's tiny ears. Or perhaps she wondered at the things he did as he grew—like discussing deep theological mysteries at age twelve—things that showed her how the baby who had once existed only within the bounds of her person was becoming an unrepeatable person of his own. I have pondered this question in my heart: How does something so internal become so external?

It makes me think of Mother Church. She nurtures the souls of her children in secret silence, and then those children "go forth" into the world, as the priest commissions us at the end of every Mass.

My motherhood, too, begins as an internal operation, particularly in those first months between conception and birth. My pregnancies were like a marvelous, growing secret that only I could fully experience. Then, when my babies became *externally* tangible to the world—as a result of concrete labor on my part—the *internal* part became more *in*tangible. But the bond still exists.

With both of my daughters I felt a mysterious but powerful bond during their infancy that caused my body to know when she needed to nurse or to sleep. That internal bond has lasted through the dance of parenting in which the invisible relationship is the force behind every visible touch and gesture—like the closeness I feel when I wear my child snuggled against my body in the wrap— and every audible exchange. There is something internal that gives it all meaning.

I believe that our Church mothers us in these mysterious, hidden ways, too. So much of my spiritual growth has been invisible to others, just as gestation of people or germination of seeds happens out of sight, but with very visible results. The private details of our conversion stories, the internal experiences and the whispers of the Holy Spirit that guide us, happen in the depths of our hearts. St.

Edith Stein put it well. She was born a Jew and became an atheist before converting to Catholicism. But she described her conversion simply as "my secret to me."[20]

The sacraments are a great example of invisible realities with external effects! These are remarkable "outward signs instituted by Christ to give grace" on the invisible level: the water of baptism, the words of absolution, the oil of anointing,[21]—and of course, the bread and wine of the Eucharist that becomes the Body of Christ. This sacrament strikes me as similarly internal, something full of life that is hidden in a marvelous, mysterious way and that actually physically feeds me.

Of course, all these musings didn't happen immediately after Communion last week. No, I am a mom, and when I returned to my pew I had to calm my wriggling two-and-a-half-year-old! But later, when I was nursing my infant at home in my inner room, then the ideas had some fertile quiet in which to germinate. While I fed my baby, my Mother Church fed my mind and soul as I pondered all of this.

Reflecting on the hidden operations of Mother Church makes me realize that, although so much of my work of mothering is invisible, it is still some of the most important work that anyone will ever do.

- What elements of Rachel's story resonate with your own? What touched, surprised, or inspired you about her reflection?

- Take a few moments to ponder or journal about how you have experienced the Church's motherly "creation" in your life. Then, turn to the study guide on page 109 for further reflection from the lives of the saints, the teaching of the Church, the liturgy, and the sacraments.

CHAPTER TWO ··· Mothers Care

I remember my mom unloading the dishwasher. Every morning, usually before the rest of us woke up, she emptied it out and restocked the kitchen cabinets for the day. At the crack of dawn, Mom was already putting herself at our service, making sure we had what we needed to start the day. The image is clear in my mind because there were a few mornings when I was up early enough to witness the ritual and to lend a hand.

Of course, she also did laundry and prepared meals and cleaned the house and ran errands and organized supplies and volunteered at the food co-op and worked at church and packed my dad's lunch for thirty-eight years and homeschooled us and led Bible studies and helped my grandma and scheduled dentist appointments and made Play-Doh from scratch. She still does many of these things, in fact. But the image of her at the dishwasher resonates with me in a particular way.

Perhaps it's because I remember thinking, one particular morning, how futile it seemed. This machine was never *really* empty. Day after day, my devoted mother would bend over the device and remove its contents. And night after night, it would be full again. The dirty dishes just kept coming. It's the sort of relentless onslaught of unending, thankless work that could cause a workers' union to go on strike. This perpetual task offered no weekend or holiday reprieve. Quite the opposite, in fact. Those were the times when the machine might run twice a day.

But there's one thing I can't remember. I have no recollection of my mother ever complaining about it. I can't conjure up the memory of an exasperated sigh or a disgruntled groan. She's not the one who planted the idea of futility in my mind. My mother has always done this duty, and all of her maternal tasks, with patient generosity. I wish I could say the same about myself.

Since stepping into the role of mother, I have been continually surprised by the amount of unexpected duties and demands that have filled my life. Of course I expected to be changing diapers and feeding the family, but the little requests of my crew never cease to catch me off guard. There are countless things for which my young children need my help: pouring the milk, scrubbing a neck, zipping a jacket, reaching a toy, putting on a Band-Aid, finding their socks, combing their hair, answering their questions about the world, and reminding them not to put crayons in their ears.

The caring never ends. As soon as I help my five-year-old get the lid off the glue stick, my two-year-old needs to be rescued from underneath a toppled rocking horse. While I am in the process of getting my four-year-old settled in with breakfast, the baby spits up all over himself and needs a change. When my seven-year-old wants to write a story, I have to get the pencil sharpener down from its safe location on high and then distract the toddler who wants to sharpen her finger.

These unending duties often frustrate me. Too often, I heave a sigh and shake my head—or worse—when I have to move from one task to the next without a moment's rest. But for all the frustration, when I step back and think for a moment, I realize that these little opportunities to serve are the meat of my motherhood. It's true that I have a noble, God-given mission as a co-creator of new life, but it's also true that this noble mission is lived out in the daily details.

These details, I suspect, have a lot to do with the reason why many women succumb to the worldly idea that motherhood is a meaningless chore. When they see only the work that's involved in mothering, it's not a surprise that some women opt for different work and opt out of having children. Let's be honest: the thought of folding children's laundry day in and day out, or wiping up spills or cleaning potty seats, doesn't thrill anyone. Buying groceries that will be quickly consumed, emptying dishwashers that will just fill up again, and tidying rooms that will be messy in minutes can ring of futility if we don't put this all in proper context.

Thank goodness, the Church helps us to keep our eyes on the bigger picture.

Mother Church Cares

Not only does the Church *tell* us that motherhood is an important mission; she also *shows* us that this mission is often expressed through scores of tiny, hidden tasks. We have seen how the Church's motherhood is manifested beautifully as she creates a new life for men and women through baptism and the other sacraments. This is an obvious and noble part of her maternal activity. But she doesn't stop there. The Church is also committed to the ongoing care of her children.

As a mother, I cook, clean, run errands, dress and groom children, remind, organize, shop, fix, and do some work that helps supplement our family income. The Church also has her daily tasks, meetings and councils, structures and systems, that keep the whole operation running. She too has to be responsible and pay the bills. None of this is glamorous, but it is all priceless. Like us, the Church has to be involved in the nitty-gritty daily details, the mundane and routine elements that are absolutely essential and totally nonglorious.

Think about the local Catholic parish, for example. The sacraments we receive in our own communities happen because we have a parish at which to receive them. All the spiritual benefits we enjoy as parish members exist because we have a parish in the first place. But consider all the routine logistics that go into making a Catholic parish possible. Each individual parish is run by a pastor, who is ordained, appointed, and supported by the bishop or arch-bishop of the diocese. The pope, who is pastor of the whole church, appoints both bishops and archbishops who are the pastors of their dioceses. This all happens not so much by way of miracle or mystery but because ministers of the Church exert their time and energy to know their flocks and their needs and to make the decisions and initiate the tasks that respond accordingly.

Once a parish is established and a pastor assigned, that parish has to operate according to the size and mission of the community. There is the need for a staff, which means (among other things) the need for offices, along with desks, computers, and phones. Someone has to obtain those things and set them up, and someone has to make sure they get fixed when they break. The bathrooms have to be cleaned, the pews have to be tidied after Mass, the schedules for the Eucharistic ministers must be made and distributed, the meetings advertised in the bulletin, the photocopies made for the religious education classes, and the coffee pot in the break room must be refilled from time to time.

These piddly details really are part of the grand mission of Mother Church! She couldn't mother us properly without them. Each little chore is a piece of the puzzle that makes up the big picture of our life of faith. And we should never be ungrateful for the systems that get these chores done.

Some people hold the belief that the existence of "earthly," organizational systems in the Catholic Church implies that it isn't really Christ's Church. Somehow, they have the mistaken idea that everything the Church does should be purely spiritual. They take offense at the minutiae involved in the Church's mission, at the offices and structures that keep her running, at the collection baskets that circulate during the offertory. Some people even conclude that an organized Church itself is unnecessary. But this is like expecting a mother to raise her children without actually caring for them.

Giving birth is only the beginning! We nurture our families through the structure of our homes (granted, some of us have better organizational systems in place than others). The Church nurtures us in a similar way.

This is an important point for appreciating the United States Conference of Catholic Bishops (USCCB), for example. This is a centralized "headquarters" that helps to promote the work of the Church in the United States. I have visited the facility in Washington, DC, and was impressed by the diversity of operations that this ecclesiastical body undertakes. There are thirty-one departments (called offices) in the system that help to address a vast array of issues. Pro-life Activities; Migration and Refugee Services; Laity, Marriage, Family Life, and Youth; Ecumenical and Interreligious; Clergy, Consecrated Life, and Vocations; and Catholic Education are just some of the offices within the USCCB. Local dioceses and parishes benefit from the efforts of the USCCB, as well as individuals. Anyone can visit the USCCB website, for example, to make use of their liturgical resources or to learn what initiatives the Church is undertaking around the country or the world.

The USCCB also promulgates documents and teachings that help respond to issues of special pastoral concern. Their 2009 letter "Marriage: Love and Life in the Divine Plan" and their document "Best Practices for Shared Parishes: So That They May All Be One" are two examples, but the list of their writings is long and diverse. Just the creation of one of these letters is a major undertaking that requires many meetings and deliberations, as well as the work of the writers, editors, and publishers.

But the USCCB is only one of many ecclesiastical bodies that offer written guidance for the faithful. Imagine how much collaboration and editing must have gone into something as universal as the *Catechism of the Catholic Church,* which went through ten drafts and "was the object of extensive consultation among all

Catholic Bishops, their Episcopal Conferences or Synods, and of theological and catechetical institutes."[22]

While the American Church in particular benefits from the presence of the USCCB, the Roman Curia exists to serve the global Church. As such, it has an even larger task on its shoulders, and it also carries a more universal authority. Due in large part to lopsided media portrayals, many people believe that the Curia is merely a messy web of bureaucratic inefficiency that just distracts from the spiritual mission of the bride of Christ. But that's not true. While it would be naïve to suggest that these ecclesiastical offices all operate with perfect precision and productivity, it would also be wrong to pretend that they are extraneous or useless to the faithful.

The document *Christus Dominus* explains the Roman Curia in this way:

> In exercising supreme, full, and immediate power in the universal Church, the Roman pontiff makes use of the departments of the Roman Curia which, therefore, perform their duties in his name and with his authority for the good of the churches and in the service of the sacred pastors.[23]

These departments exist to help the pope carry out the concrete *tasks* of the Church. The analogy isn't exact, but we can think of this in family terms. Mother Church helps the Holy Father get things done just as so many mothers help their children's fathers carry out the concrete *tasks* of the family.

Of course it differs from family to family, but rare is the mother who does not have some collection of practical responsibilities on her plate. Whether it be balancing the checkbook (like the Prefecture for the Economic Affairs of the Holy See), establishing and overseeing the household rules (like the Pontifical Commission for the Protection of Minors), preserving family history (like the Papal Archives), involving the kids in community service (like the Office of Papal Charities), making sure everyone is on track at school (like the Congregation for Catholic Education), or keeping family traditions alive (like the Pontifical Commission for the Cultural Heritage of the Church), mothers are busy making family life function.

The Church does the same through her curial councils (of which there are twelve), congregations (nine), offices (five), tribunals (three), commissions (eight), academies (eleven), and committees (two). I have six children, and I would lose my wits without a few good methods of household management. I can only imagine what would happen if I had 1.2 billion children and no management system. We really should thank God for the care we receive, trickle-down though it may be, from the Vatican. In fact, the nation of the Vatican exists to serve us and the entire Church:

> In the exercise of his task at the service of the Church throughout the world, the Pope is assisted by a series of bodies brought together under the name of Roman Curia. The Curia is not to be confused with the government of a State. The Pope is, indeed, also a Head of State, the Head of the smallest State in the world, the Vatican City; but the only reason for the existence of this tiny State is to guarantee the freedom the Pope needs for the exercise of his function as Supreme Pastor of the Catholic Church. It is in this specific function that he is assisted by the Roman Curia. The Curia is made up of different dicasteries which take care of different aspects of the life of the Church and of her relations with the realities of the world.[24]

My experience with the Pontifical Council for the Laity (PCL) confirmed for me the importance of the Vatican offices. In the introduction, I mentioned a private audience with Pope Francis as part of a gathering commemorating the anniversary of *Mulieris Dignitatem*. This seminar was sponsored in Rome by the PCL. Along with one hundred women from around the world, I had been invited to participate in this conference. It happened to occur when my fourth child was four months old, but the president of the Council, Cardinal Stanisław Ryłko, gave me permission to bring her along. I loved that. It helped me realize that this curial council was not an impersonal ecclesiastical machine; it was a Church ministry led by a welcoming man.

The seminar took place at an "off campus" Vatican facility called the Palazzo San Callisto. This was a beautiful conference center, accented by marble porticoes and cobblestone courtyards, in the neighborhood of the ancient Basilica of Santa Maria in Trastevere. Here I gathered with married, single, and consecrated women from all over the globe, representing twenty-four different countries, to discuss the themes of Pope St. John Paul II's document and to brainstorm concrete plans of action. A few husbands and fathers as well as some monsignors also joined our ranks for this three-day session. Teachers, nurses, social workers, scientists, missionaries, journalists, lawyers, students, doctors, catechists, professors, artists, theologians, and, of course, mothers all shared their insights and ideas.

Being amid this tangible display of the universality of Catholicism was like stepping right into the heart of Mother Church. The fact that we were on Vatican property, participating in the work of the Curia, also added to this sense of connection with the entire Church. Until this point, I had never thought much about pontifical councils, for good or for ill. But what impressions I had gathered left a vague sense of dry, bureaucratic boredom. But my encounter with the PCL was anything but dry or boring. This experience was energizing and inspiring. It bolstered my faith and sent me forth with a mission (of which this book is a part!). The seminar created friendships and concrete resolutions. It empowered women to return to their homes with new zeal for the mission of the Church. Even now, the fruits of this event continue to unfold.

None of this would have happened if the PCL hadn't invited, gathered, welcomed, and hosted this company of women from around the world. This was a maternal undertaking, to be sure! The planning and preparation began well in advance of the session itself. The reserving of rooms and printing of programs, the organization of talks and sessions and translators, the ordering of pastries and orange juice, the chartering of a bus to take us to meet Pope Francis—all of this had to be done by the staff of the Council. All of this work, this tiny work, had to be carried out by caring hands and hearts.

The centralized structure of the Roman Curia made this possible. In fact, this system enables us *all* to maintain a kind of family connection. We may live in different continents, speak different languages, and have different pressing concerns, but we are all united through our belonging to the universal (i.e., catholic) Church. Without the sense of home base that we find in Rome, our feeling of family would be without root or substance. We would be members of a thousand little churches, but we would lack a sense of connection to the larger family. We would each tend to stray off in different directions, instead of staying connected to the traditions, the practices, and the teachings that are meant for us all.

Perhaps St. Peter's Square gives us the best image to sum up the maternal nature of the Vatican. The great twelfth-century architect Gian Lorenzo Bernini conceived of this space as an image of "the enfolding arms of Mother Church."[25] Outside the grand Basilica of St. Peter, the piazza is marked by 284 columns that surround a space nearly 350 yards long and 260 yards wide. These columns present an image that literally looks like outstretched arms, circling around in a hug. As Bernini said, "Considering that Saint Peter's is almost the matrix of all the churches, its portico had to give an open-armed, maternal welcome."[26]

This welcome is real. It's universal. And it's tangible. Without the little details of management and care, the Church wouldn't be much of a mother. It's easy to underestimate, overlook, or take for granted these unloading-the-dishwasher type tasks. But in truth, they make all the difference.

Another Mother's Voice: Deborah's Story

Deborah is a foster mom and the adoptive mother of two sons.
The Church has been like a mother to me in many ways—accepting me, teaching me, keeping me from harm. But perhaps the biggest influence Mother Church has had on my life is the way she brought me to my own motherhood.

The journey took a while. First, when I had to face infertility problems, the Church helped me change my attitude toward motherhood. Before, when I assumed I could conceive easily, being a mother was very much about me. *I* wanted to play the mother role, *I* wanted a child, *I* was entitled to children as if they were something to be possessed or owned. It was really all about fulfilling my desires and wants. Only in grappling with my feelings through infertility did I become aware of these unconscious attitudes.

As I prayed and grieved, the Church helped me view motherhood as a loving stewardship, rather than ownership, and helped me realize that children were a pure gift from God to *all* of humanity, not just their parents. The wisdom of the Church helped me see that these young people belonged to God and to themselves. As parents, if we are entrusted with their care for a period of time, that is our opportunity to contribute a loving service, not just for the children, but for the whole body of Christ.

During this process when my husband and I were coming to accept infertility, the Church transformed me through her teachings on spiritual motherhood. She helped me understand the importance of helping those children who were in my life as nieces or nephews, godchildren, or just children of friends.

The biggest opportunity I had to live this type of motherhood was when my sister-in-law and brother-in-law came to live with us along with our two young nieces. In all honesty, I don't feel that I performed at all well during this time. I was experiencing, perhaps for the first time, the fact that "loving service" wasn't as sweet or simple as it sounded. Unconditional love—difficult? Who knew?

It was also the Church that challenged me to pursue motherhood when I no longer wanted to. After a turbulent two-and-a-half years of living with family in our home, I certainly felt how much easier life could be as a childless couple. I'm not saying better, but definitely easier. I no longer felt any desire to have children. In truth, I didn't want them.

By the grace of God, my husband did not share my sentiments. And the Church helped redirect my thinking, too. As Pope St. John Paul II said at a gathering of families, "To couples who cannot have children of their own I say: you are no less loved by God; your love for each other is complete and fruitful when it is open to others, to the needs of the apostolate, to the needs of the poor, to the needs of orphans, to the needs of the world."[27] We began to discern how we as a couple were called to be fruitful.

I knew that God had blessed me with a rich faith, a good marriage, and a good home with rooms to spare and share. And I understood that these gifts were not just for my benefit alone. In addition, our experience living with family, though very challenging, had opened our minds to the possibility of having a positive impact on a child's life, even if he or she wasn't going to be with us forever. One Scripture verse in particular really spoke to my heart: "Religion that is pure and undefiled before God, the Father, is this: to care for orphans and widows in their distress, and to keep oneself unstained by the world" (James 1:27). So we discerned that we could minister to the vulnerable children in foster care and we could provide a safe and caring home for as long as they needed it.

We've now had eight children placed with us over the past two-and-a-half years. Six of those children have come and gone, but two of them remained with us; we adopted both of our sons after first welcoming them into our home as foster children. So the Church is really responsible for my becoming a mother, and she continues to shape and support my motherhood by providing the grace through the sacraments to heal my heart when we have to let go of a child, by extending forgiveness for my shortcomings as a mother, and by giving me the continual challenge and encouragement—despite the difficulties we face as parents and participants of the foster-care system—to carry on and be open to welcoming children into my home and into my heart.

- What elements of Deborah's story resonate with your own? What touched, surprised, or inspired you about her reflection?

- Take a few moments to ponder or journal about how you have experienced the Church's motherly "care" in your life. Then, turn to the study guide on page 111 for further reflection from the lives of the saints, the teaching of the Church, the liturgy, and the sacraments.

CHAPTER THREE ··· Mothers Teach

As I was slicing onions the other day, my four-year-old daughter asked if she could watch. I told her she was welcome to watch, but that she'd have to be prepared for the tears. She hauled a chair over to the counter, climbed aboard, and looked on as I cried and chopped. Then she asked me, "Mom, why are you holding your hand like that?" She wasn't referring to the hand with the knife, but the other one. My fingertips were perched atop the onion and my knuckles were pushed forward, just in front of my nails. I glanced down. It did look a little awkward.

"Nonna taught me to do this," I replied. "It keeps my fingers safe while I'm using a knife." The memory came back to me of spending an afternoon with my now-centenarian grandmother, learning how to make her spaghetti sauce and a few other favorite family dishes. I was in my early twenties at the time, and anything but a proficient cook; the only dinner I had ever served to friends left one in hives and the other in the restroom for the remainder of the evening.

But Grandma was undaunted. She welcomed me into the kitchen—*her* favorite place—and set out to teach me a few things I needed to know. Along with the family recipes (which I wrote down to preserve for posterity), she gave me a tutorial in some essential culinary skills—like how to chop onions without chopping your fingers, for example. After watching me risk such an event, she instructed me on a better method.

"If you push your knuckles up and out, you'll protect your fingertips," she explained. Then she demonstrated. I remember the sight of the knife next to her slightly arthritic knuckles as she minced onions like a master chef. I also remember the difficulty I had trying to carry out her instructions. But she coached me, and I practiced, and now nearly two decades later the whole thing has become so second nature to me that it took a four-year-old to remind me that once upon a time I didn't know how to slice onions.

What else didn't I know once upon a time? Well, everything, really: how to talk, how to walk, how to get dressed, and all the other basic how-tos. But more than that, I had to learn how to relate to people, how to be polite, how to defend myself, and how to stick up for others. I had to learn what was safe and what was dangerous, what was good and what was evil, what was kind and respectful and just, and what was just plain wrong.

I had to learn what my gifts and strengths were, and how I could acknowledge and improve upon my weaknesses. I had to learn how to manage my money and keep my room clean and roller skate and thread a needle and say my prayers and fold my shirts and share my belongings with my siblings and friends—the big, the small, and everything in between. And so much of this I learned from my mother.

Pope Francis explains this lifelong educational exchange between mother and child in the context of love:

> A good mother can recognize everything that God is bringing about in her children, she listens to their concerns and learns from them. The spirit of love which reigns in a family guides both mother and child in their conversations; therein they teach and learn, experience correction and grow in appreciation of what is good.[28]

Of course my grandparents, aunts, uncles, siblings, and friends were all major influences in my life who also helped me to "grow in appreciation of what is good" through their love. And it would be impossible to determine which of my parents taught me "more" since they were both constantly teaching me whatever I needed to know. But the fact is that my mother's presence and guidance, which thankfully continue to this day, have not only enabled me to function, but have also profoundly shaped me as a person.

As mothers, this is what we do for our children. We shape them into the people they become, one small lesson at a time.

Sometimes we forget how much there is to teach them. So often, my children ask questions that remind me what I simply assumed they knew. This reality is manifested in both simple and profound ways:

"What for wunch, Mama?" asks my two-year-old.

"Meatloaf," I reply.

"What's meatwoaf?" she asks. Oh yes. There's a first time for everything, I remember. Even meatloaf.

Or, on the grander scale: "Where is Daddy going?" my son wants to know as Joe gets dressed up and prepares to leave.

"He's going to a funeral."

"What's a funeral?" Oh. Right. Funerals. I wasn't planning on explaining this tonight, but here goes. And suddenly I am in the middle of a dialogue about death and eternal life and grief and mortuary science.

This is what we do. We answer the questions as they come up, and we teach the skills as they are needed. But this is not all we do. As mothers, we aren't just playing defense as our children's ignorance is thrown our way. We are also called to be on the offensive, deliberately enacting strategies to form and shape our children.

This happens both through our example and through our deliberate teaching. It's important to remember that our children learn from us even when we aren't giving a "lesson." What we do and how we behave in their presence and respond to their needs tends to impact them more than what we say. This is why the Church reminds us that "parents have a grave responsibility to give good example to their children" (CCC, 2223).

When I come face-to-face with my impatience and selfishness, that responsibility can feel terribly daunting. But the *Catechism* continues with these comforting words: "By knowing how to acknowledge their own failings to their children, parents will be better able to guide and correct them" (CCC, 2223). We are not perfect mothers, because we are not perfect people. But even the process of humbly acknowledging this fact to our children is part of their education.

We are called to teach our sons and daughters values and virtues that will help them deal with whatever life should bring and then to continue to accompany them through adulthood. We are called to direct them, to influence their choices, and to help form their consciences. We are called to assist their development into happy, healthy, holy people.

To this extent, our influence as mothers cannot be underestimated. As St. Madeleine Sophie Barat wrote already in the early nineteenth century:

> We must no longer count on men to preserve the Faith.... Between women and God is often arranged the eternal salvation of husbands and sons.... A woman cannot remain neutral in the world; she too is set for the fall and resurrection of many.[29]

Of course we hope to assist our children on the path to the "resurrection" of eternal life. The *Catechism* offers us some inspiring—and challenging—directives for how to approach this duty, telling us that, as parents, we hold the primary responsibility for educating our children. As such, we are called to establish a home environment where "tenderness, forgiveness, respect, fidelity, and disinterested service are the rule" (CCC, 2223). The *Catechism* goes on to propose that our homes are especially well suited to educating our children in a life of virtue through training in "self-denial, sound judgment, and self-mastery" (CCC, 2223)—traits that are all necessary to experience authentic freedom.

Some of us learned these lessons from our parents, some of us figured them out along the way, and perhaps others are just now encountering them. Whatever the case, it is up to us to pass along to our children a proper "education in the virtues," along with all the other bits and pieces of knowledge that we share with them throughout their lives.

As my daughter asked me about onions that day, I thought of how beautiful it was to be able to teach her what my grandmother had taught me. I thought about the gift of my grandmother's culinary experience living on in my daughter, and possibly in her daughter and her granddaughter, and so on. In this sense, my grandma has helped me educate my daughter. I am simply passing along what I have learned.

I do this for the bigger things, too. I pass on to my children what I have learned about faith and family and friendship. I educate them by sharing the wisdom that has been shared with me, or that I have gained through experience.

This is just what Mother Church does for all of us. "Because she is our mother," the *Catechism* tells us, "she is also our teacher in the faith" (CCC, 169).

Mother Church Teaches

The Church has two thousand years of experience. Two millennia of cumulative wisdom. And, to top it off, the promise of Christ that, "when the Spirit of truth comes, he will guide you into all the truth" (John 16:13). My grandmother has much to share from the fruit of her full century on this earth, but how much more does the Church have to share from the fruit of her own greatly advanced age! Not only has the Church lived through enough history to learn a great deal, but she has done so under the guidance of the Holy Spirit. This is a mother who knows what she's talking about.

In our culture today, however, many people are skeptical of her voice. Perhaps this is partly because too often we assume that newer equals better. New clothes, new cars, new houses, and new gadgets all have their appeal. But if we aren't careful, we can fall into the trap of applying the principle across the board. We can begin to develop a kind of disdain for that which is old, labeling it dull or unappealing at best, and at worst dismissing it as obsolete without a fair hearing.

Mother Church deserves more respect than this. Just as it would be foolish to deny the dignity and sagacity of our elders, so too it would be unwise to dismiss the value of the traditions of the Church. The Church does what she does with good reason. Instead of writing her off as irrelevant or archaic, we would do well to heed her example and follow her advice. She has our best interest at heart, after all, and thanks to her vast history—in which God's revelation in Christ has been passed to us through the collective wisdom of countless holy men and women—she has treasures within her storehouse that can guide us more surely than the counsel of any one individual.

Our children may think they are wiser than we are. But we know that, for all their intelligence, they still lack the wisdom that comes only from experience. Thus, as a general principle, we expect children to be obedient to their parents for the children's own sake. The same idea applies when it comes to the traditions and teachings of the Church.

In his book, *A Shepherd Speaks*, Bishop Fabian Bruskewitz explains this idea:

> Mothers, as a general rule, command obedience in those things that are for the welfare of their children. Good mothers are never capricious, tyrannical, or cruel in what they demand of their offspring. And devoted children love and cherish their mothers and treat them with respect and

deference. The obedience that the Church asks of her children is simply to keep them better joined to her divine Spouse, Christ Jesus.... It is only when we see the Church as our true and loving mother that our obedience makes sense and changes from something extrinsic and difficult into a happy listening to the very voice of our Savior, Who said to His Catholic Church: "Who hears you hears me."[30]

It's important to distinguish between what Mother Church actually says to us through her teachings, and what some of her children choose to do. The history of the Church is marred by certain sons and daughters who have abused their mother's name. Straying from her teachings and her values, these wayward children have charted their own course in the name of Catholicism, leaving a trail of misery, violence, or devastation in their wake. This is the cost of human freedom. But we cannot hold this against the Church any more than we can condemn a mother whose child has gone astray. It would be ridiculous to imprison a mother because her grown son is a thief.

Thus, we can turn with confidence to the true teachings of Mother Church, seeking wisdom and guidance therein. Teaching is, in fact, part of the fundamental reason for the Church's existence. "As a mother who teaches her children to speak and so to understand and communicate," the *Catechism* tells us, "the Church our Mother teaches us the language of faith in order to introduce us to the understanding and the life of faith" (CCC, 171).

We learn the language of faith from the Word of God communicated in Sacred Tradition and Sacred Scripture. The *Catechism* explains how the Gospel comes to us both orally and in writing.[31] The oral dimension of the Gospel was handed on to us by the apostles. Through the words they preached, through their lived example, and through the institutions they set up, the apostles passed on what they had received from Jesus. His way of life, his works, and the inspiration of his Holy Spirit provided them with all the material of the Gospel. Later, this same Holy Spirit also inspired certain apostles and their associates to put the message of the Gospel in writing. The Magisterium of the Catholic Church is the teaching office of the Church that protects and explains these oral and written teachings that we collectively refer to as the deposit of faith.

So, using the (imperfect) analogy of chopping onions, Sacred Tradition is like the actual method of safe onion chopping. Sacred Scripture is like the recipe cards I made with written reference to the method, and Grandma is like the Magisterium.

Tradition is what is done, what has been done, and what continues to get done, regardless of the century or the location: onions get chopped with protruding knuckles; the Eucharist gets celebrated with bread and wine. (In the case of the Eucharist, of course, the tradition is divinely established. Not so in the case of the onions!) "Through Tradition," the *Catechism* states, "'the Church, in her doctrine, life, and worship perpetuates and transmits to every generation all that she herself is, all that she believes'" (*CCC*, 78). The Church shares herself with us by sharing her Sacred Tradition with us. Tradition is essential to who she is and what she believes. And it came before any written record was made of any of it.

Scripture goes hand in hand with Tradition. It contains the written record of the existence of the Tradition. Therefore, Scripture comes after Tradition is already in place. The recipe card says, "Sauté one cup of minced onion, chopped in the Giambrone method." The written notes assume that the reader knows how to practice the Giambrone method. So in order to fully understand the recipe card, you have to know the "tradition" that preceded it.

Similarly, Luke's Gospel says, "Then he took a loaf of bread, and when he had given thanks, he broke it and gave it to them, saying, 'This is my body, which is given for you. Do this in remembrance of me'" (Luke 22:19). The Church has been doing this in remembrance of Jesus ever since the Last Supper. It is part of her Sacred Tradition. Because of this, the Church knows what to say and what to do when she celebrates the Eucharist.

It's important to recognize that the Church was practicing all of this *before the books of the New Testament were written.* These practices were put down in writing later (in Scripture) to help preserve the practice for the future, since the written reference makes the most sense in the context of the constant practice. As the *Catechism* teaches, "Sacred Tradition and Sacred Scripture, then, are bound closely together and communicate one with the other" (CCC, 80). Both Scripture and Tradition have the same divine source and join together to form one deposit of faith. Together they manifest the mystery of Christ to the Church. Yet, they remain two different but complimentary methods of transmitting the Gospel. Sacred Scripture is "the speech of God as it is put down in writing under the breath of the Holy Spirit" (CCC, 81), while Sacred Tradition passes on the Word of God that was entrusted to the apostles by Jesus and the Holy Spirit through teaching and practice.

Now, when it comes to actually carrying out the practice, the Magisterium is an incredible gift. This teaching authority of the Church helps the believer to make the most of the deposit of faith.

So Grandma, whose mother taught her to chop onions, tells me about the method, shows me how to do it, and guides me as I learn it for myself. Without her, it would be much harder for me to learn this family tradition (such as if I had learned of it through a different source, like a letter or journal). Similarly, the Magisterium helps us follow Tradition and be faithful to Scripture. The *Catechism* explains it in in this way:

> Yet this Magisterium is not superior to the Word of God,
> but is its servant. It teaches only what has been handed on

to it. At the divine command and with the help of the Holy Spirit, it listens to this devotedly, guards it with dedication, and expounds it faithfully. All that it proposes for belief as being divinely revealed is drawn from this single deposit of faith." (CCC, 86)

The very fact that I can quote the *Catechism* when I am explaining the deposit of faith is thanks to the Magisterium—the Magisterium produced the *Catechism* for us! This Magisterium has the duty to interpret authentically and to explain God's Word to us, both in its written form and in the form of Sacred Tradition. As the official teaching office of the Church, the Magisterium alone has this special authority, carried out in the name of Christ. In practice, it is always the bishops of the Church together with the successor of St. Peter, the pope, who comprise the Magisterium.[32]

So, the *Catechism* was the fruit of the collaboration between the bishops and the pope (St. John Paul II), who together hold the magisterial authority of the Church. This setup, by the way, was part of Jesus's original plan. He's the one who established the structure and the authority of the pope and the bishops.

In Matthew's Gospel, we hear how closely connected the Church is to the pope. "And I tell you, you are Peter," Jesus said, "and on this rock I will build my church" (Matthew 16:18). The name "Peter" means rock, and here Jesus emphasizes that this man is the solid foundation underlying the Church, *Christ's* Church. Jesus specifically says this is "his" Church. It's not Peter's Church. It's Jesus's Church. But Peter is the rock on which it's built.

In the same passage we learn that Jesus told Peter, "I will give you the keys of the kingdom of heaven" (Matthew 16:19). In other words, Jesus gave Peter a very special kind of authority on earth. And Peter, in turn, passed this authority on to his successor, and then to the next successor, and so on for all 266 popes (to date).

The other apostles also passed on their authority to their successors. The office of every bishop in the Catholic Church stretches back to one of the twelve apostles who, like Peter, received from Jesus the power to "bind and loose" (see Matthew 18:18). It's this steady stream of bishops that allows us to call the Catholic Church "apostolic." Catholics enjoy the confidence of being part of this apostolic succession, and can thus put a great deal of trust in the education they receive from the loving hands of Mother Church.

Another Mother's Voice: Sandy's Story

Sandy is the mother of two teenage sons and one adult son.

My upbringing was difficult. Two years before I was born, my family lost my brother to crib death. His death created a wedge in the family from which they were never able to recover.

My mother was perhaps the most deeply affected. I love her very much, yet her struggles made it hard for her to be available to her family. I'm sure she did the best she was able to. However, I felt as prepared for life as if I'd been raised by wolves. My difficult upbringing left huge gaps in my view of what it means to be a mother.

Looking back, I remember being alone a lot, and being a bit envious of my friends who had moms who were usually home—typical suburban moms, cooking, cleaning, and making the best refrigerator pickles I'd ever had in my life. Now *those* were the moms to have.

What I didn't notice at the time were the boundaries and expectations these moms placed on their kids. They couldn't always come out to play, and they couldn't stay out as late as I did. They were being formed in ways I was not.

Which brings me to my point. Like my friends' attentive moms, the Church has been my mother in ways I didn't expect or necessarily want. For my own security and happiness, she makes me do things I don't want to do. She gives guidelines to my conduct, and as with any good mother, she does so in ways I have needed, whether I like it or not.

When I became Catholic, the Church became the mother that taught me personal responsibility and self-denial, humility, persistence, and perseverance. Mother Church has been the one to challenge me to stretch and learn beyond what I thought I could do. And I've grown to love and appreciate her, even when I don't understand the reasons behind her teachings.

My motherhood, too, has been shaped by the Church. I met my oldest son's father when I had just graduated high school—which was a miracle in itself. We got married when I was nineteen. Then came my son, and his first Christmas. I remember singing carols and thinking about Mary and wondering if she knew what would become of her son. Though I was not yet Catholic, I felt somehow united to her in that moment.

As I contemplated, and cried, and wondered what would become of *my* son, suddenly the weight of how unprepared I was for motherhood crushed me. I thought of all that I had not learned but now needed to know. I knew nothing. Zero. I didn't know how to cook, clean, pay bills, much less be a loving, nurturing mother. My head was spinning, and this precious, perfect, beautiful baby boy slept in my arms. My early experiences left me feeling like I was not cut out for motherhood. I felt empty and unfulfilled, as if no one else could possibly understand me.

Time passed. I got a divorce, and later met and married Jamie. When our first son (my second son) was born thirteen years ago, we knew we wanted to have him baptized, but we weren't sure where. We went to a handful of churches together, but nothing felt right.

Then we decided we would try a Catholic church. When the priest said, "Lord, I am not worthy to receive you" and meant it, I completely understood. I knew then that this was the place for us.

It took a little longer before I started RCIA. I think my family thought I had joined a cult, but I *knew* I was in the right place, doing the right thing. I try to keep in touch with my family, who are gradually seeing the positive changes in my life. But these changes are not my doing. They have only happened through God and by the guidance and teaching of the Church.

Despite the changes and growth in me over the years, I still fight those insecurities of not being up to the task of mothering. But when we come to Mass each Sunday, we see women in all stages of motherhood. Their faces are our faces in a few years, or a few years ago. In coming together, we share a bond in a larger family, even though we are not related.

When I feel inadequate, I think of my larger church "family" that I have as an example, and I pray. I pray the prayers Mother Church has taught me. I reach out to the saints to pray with me for my children. And I try to be open to the prompting of the Holy Spirit to guide me on this journey of motherhood.

- What elements of Sandy's story resonate with your own? What touched, surprised, or inspired you about her reflection?

- Take a few moments to ponder or journal about how you have experienced the Church's motherly "teaching" in your life. Then, turn to the study guide on page 113 for further reflection from the lives of the saints, the teaching of the Church, the liturgy, and the sacraments.

CHAPTER FOUR ··· Mothers Accept

Before I had children, I often wondered why so many parents loved to show off pictures of their kids. I was always surprised at how frequently wallet-sized photos of children occupied precious space in purses or billfolds and how frequently I was put on the spot to express my admiration for these proudly produced images.

Alongside—or even instead of—classical artwork or designer decorations on the walls of their homes, countless couples choose to adorn their houses with portraits of their children. Susie at one year, Susie at two years, Susie at three years, and on it goes. *Don't you get a little tired of looking at Susie?* I thought to myself. Apparently not.

The stereotypical annual Christmas card where yuletide wishes border a family photo also used to puzzle and even annoy me, particularly when people chose to send a picture that didn't include them. *Why just the kids?* was my interior response.

What's this fascination with the faces of our children? Why do we assume everybody else is just as taken with our kids as we are? Well, now that I have a crew of children myself, I have a theory about this. (For the record, I make a point of not sending Christmas photo cards without Joe and me in them, but I think I have come a long way in understanding and sympathizing with the phenomenon.)

I believe it's because, as parents, we see our children for who they really are. We look at them and behold their beauty, their goodness, and their inherent value. We can fully appreciate the miracle of their existence. We know them and we love them. And all of this is so crystal clear to us (on good days, anyway) that we can't help but think it's also clear to the whole world.

Alas, that usually isn't so.

In our present, fallen condition, the love we as mothers have for our children (imperfect though that love is in us) enables us to see more clearly into the window of our children's souls, beholding their God-given glory more easily than other people are able to do. The truth is, most of us fail to truly recognize the beauty in those around us. In a perfect world, untainted by sin and selfishness, we would see *everyone* with the loving eyes a godly mother has for her children. We are meant to behold everyone's dignity and value when we encounter them. Our experience as parents, perhaps, is meant in part to teach us this truth.

The compassion we feel for our children is also appropriate to feel for others. I think about the times when I have witnessed my children being rejected or left out while playing with other kids. It's hard to express the sinking feeling, the pain and concern, that this causes me as their mother. I want everyone to love my children! In these moments I struggle to understand how anyone, even a five-year-old, could not appreciate the gift of my son or daughter. But do I think of *others* that way?

Think of the agony a mother endures when one of her children is the victim of bullying. A mother sees her child's goodness and is able to overlook (in ways others do not) oddities or idiosyncrasies that make her child an easy target. As mothers we hold together the whole picture. These traits are not the sum total of who a child is, and we understand that. "He has a face only a mother could love," we sometimes say. We know that a mother's love is meant to be an absolute given, without judgment or rejection mixed in.

A mother has been built by God to love and accept her child. From the first moment that a baby begins to live inside of her body, she is designed to appreciate and embrace that new little person. Pope St. John Paul II put it beautifully in *Mulieris Dignitatem* when he said, "God entrusts the human being to [the woman] in a special way."[33] God made women to be the first ones to welcome human life into the world. Women are acceptance personified, they are the first source of all human hospitality.

As that little life grows and develops, the mother continues to accept and embrace her son or daughter. Of course a mother doesn't know "who" her child is going to be until the baby is born into the world, but she accepts the child nonetheless. Sometimes, parents are surprised to learn that their children will have special needs, physical disabilities, or lifelong health concerns. This, too, a mother is called to accept as part of her maternal hospitality.

In the case where a pregnant woman is unable (or unwilling) to take on the responsibilities of motherhood, she nonetheless must make a decision about the fate of her child. Too often, women face pressure to make an abortion decision in the case of an "imperfect" child or an unplanned pregnancy. This choice, of course, is the antithesis to maternal acceptance. Sadly, the rejection of an unborn life not only affects the child, but as more and more research indicates, the mother often suffers as well in the wake of an abortion. Society at large is thus affected not only by the loss of this new person's presence, but also by the sorrow of these suffering women.

On the other hand, by entrusting her child to the care of an adoptive family, a woman in a difficult situation can embody a kind of maternal acceptance and hospitality, accepting the suffering that is part of this personal sacrifice made out of love for her child. She thus gives life to her child and blesses society—and another family in particular—through the acceptance of her child's life. Similarly, the mother who welcomes a child into her home through adoption manifests this same maternal spirit as she literally embraces the child that God places in her life.

The welcome goes beyond accepting a new family member, however. The acceptance involves more than saying, "You can live here." Maternal acceptance embraces the entire person for his or her entire life. It means accompanying and supporting our children. It means working through problems as much as celebrating joys. It means giving our sons and daughters a taste, however imperfect, of unconditional love.

While there are sad stories of estrangement between mothers and children, these strike us as sorrowful precisely because we know it should not be so. We know deep down that, at all costs, a mother should be there for her child, and no mistake, failure, or disappointment should alienate this precious and unique relationship.

Sometimes, a son or daughter's choices bring dramatic trials to our families, such as drug addiction, imprisonment, or broken marriages. Other trials are more personal in nature—when a child rejects the faith or breaks off family ties, for example. These situations often present an even more intense test for a mother, when either she herself or her values are directly rejected or despised. But truly, a mother is at her best when her love survives these struggles. In situations like these, a mother has the chance to become the face of mercy to her children.

Mother Church Accepts

The Church, of course, is meant to be the face of mercy to the world. As Christ's body on earth, she has the mission to make divine mercy tangible and available to everyone. Pope St. John XXIII put it well in the speech that opened the Second Vatican Council, when he said that the Catholic Church desires "to show herself to the world as the loving mother of all mankind; gentle, patient, and full of tenderness and sympathy for her separated children."[34]

Who are the children separated from the Church? The list is long. It includes all those who have never belonged to the Christian family—unbaptized members of other faiths as well as people who have never professed any religion at all. Christians who are "brothers" by virtue of baptism (CCC, 818–819) but are not in full communion with the Catholic faith are imperfectly united with Mother Church, and in a sense are "separated" as well.

Of special concern are those separated by choice, Mother Church's "lost children" who have fallen away from the Catholic faith they once embraced. This separation of spiritual mother and child happens for a host of reasons. Some alienate themselves out of intellectual or spiritual pride, deliberately placing themselves outside the fold through incredulity, heresy, apostasy, or schism (CCC, 2089). Like any good parent, Mother Church does not attempt to override their will, but stands ready to welcome home the prodigal who chooses to repent.

Not all who leave the Church do so out of pride, however. Sometimes, the alienation is painful and tragic. Individuals who have suffered abuse at the hands of one of the disloyal sons of the Church certainly come to mind; these children often choose to leave under the most difficult of circumstances. Here we must recall the scriptural admonition concerning those who cause such tragedy: "It would be better for you if a millstone were hung around your neck and you were thrown into the sea than for you to cause one of these little ones to stumble" (Luke 17:2).

Lapsed Catholics who cease to practice their faith because they do not like certain Church teachings (such as those regarding contraception, abortion, or divorce) often experience a gradual spiritual alienation; some ultimately choose to leave and no longer participate in the life of the Church only after continuing in this mental or spiritual separation for a time. Others gradually allow their personal preferences or desires to draw them away because they don't feel they gain anything from Sunday Mass or because they haven't found enough personal support or welcome among the Catholic community. Still others never make a formal decision to abandon their Mother Church, but simply fade away from the practice of their faith as other cares take priority in their lives.

Whatever the case, the fact remains that the Church as mother loves and accepts *everyone*, separated or not. As an extension of Christ on earth, the Church does not pick and choose who is worthy of her love and care.

Unfortunately, however, at times individuals who claim to speak in the name of the Church do not demonstrate the patient mercy that belongs to her nature. This can happen from "on high" when a bishop or priest alienates a group or an individual through his behavior, or on the level of a lay Catholic's personal treatment of someone on the fringes of the faith. Tragically, in these cases, the separated children sense that they are unwanted instead of hearing the voice of their mother calling them back home.

This is not to suggest that the Church must never say anything that people don't want to hear. She continues to proclaim the Gospel of Christ—a message that upholds moral law and requires personal sacrifice and commitment. When a child refuses to accept the message, like a good mother the Church doesn't cater to the selfish whims of the child. Instead, she does her best to instruct and nurture her sons and daughters to bring them to enlightenment and freedom. She cannot stop them from rebelling or railing against her. But she can continue to extend her hospitality even in the midst of the storm.

So the Church, which concretely means all of her members, is called to extend a welcome precisely to those brothers and sisters that are most challenging to embrace. Pope Francis, in his letter declaring the jubilee Year of Mercy, spoke of this merciful behavior as a key characteristic for Christians:

> Jesus affirms that mercy is not only an action of the Father, it becomes a criterion for ascertaining who his true children are. In short, we are called to show mercy because mercy has first been shown to us. Pardoning offences becomes the clearest expression of merciful love, and for us Christians it is an imperative from which we cannot excuse ourselves.[35]

Jesus showed us the ultimate mercy on the cross when he suffered and died to forgive our sins and welcome us into heaven, as St. Paul says, "while we were still sinners" (Romans 5:8). Jesus didn't wait for us to become saints before he made this consummate act of love.

As Christians we cannot forget that we are the direct beneficiaries of God's mercy in Christ. The Church's constant teaching is that we are likewise called to show mercy to others. Yet, this is not always easy. Pope Francis continues:

> At times how hard it seems to forgive! And yet pardon is the instrument placed into our fragile hands to attain serenity of heart. To let go of anger, wrath, violence, and revenge are necessary conditions to living joyfully. Let us therefore heed the Apostle's exhortation: "Do not let the sun go down on your anger" (Ephesians 4:26). Above all, let us listen to the words of Jesus who made mercy an ideal of life and a criterion for the credibility of our faith: "Blessed are the merciful, for they shall obtain mercy." (Matthew 5:7)[36]

As the children of the Church, we are meant to be witnesses to mercy! This challenge reaches right into our own homes. In our relationships with our families, with all of the trials and challenges they bring, we are called to manifest forgiveness and acceptance. This is what Mother Church teaches us to do, not just by her words, but also by her example.

During a Wednesday general audience, the Holy Father expounded on this theme:

> And thus the Church conducts herself like Jesus. She does not teach theoretical lessons on love, on mercy. She does not spread to the world a philosophy, a way of wisdom.... Of course, Christianity is also all of this, but as an effect, by reflex. Mother Church, like Jesus, teaches by example, and the words serve to illuminate the meaning of her actions.[37]

We look to the Church as our model. "Mercy is the very founda-tion of the Church's life,"[38] Pope Francis says. In particular, in the lives of her saints, we find countless examples of how she has made mercy concrete. These holy sons and daughters of the Church, these members of the People of God throughout history, bear testi-mony to the true generosity and open acceptance of the Church. They serve as models for us as we seek to practice these virtues that are at the heart of our faith.

Perhaps the most helpful way to distill the vast history of prac-tical mercy in the Church is to consider how her children have exemplified the corporal and spiritual works of mercy. These two categories distinguish between acts of service on a physical, bodily level, and less visible, more spiritual acts. Each category is seven in number. The corporal works of mercy are to feed the hungry, give drink to the thirsty, clothe the naked, shelter the homeless, visit the imprisoned, care for the sick, and bury the dead. The spiritual works of mercy are to instruct the ignorant, counsel the doubtful, admonish sinners, bear wrongs patiently, forgive offences willingly, comfort the afflicted, and pray for the living and the dead.

How maternal are all of these works of mercy! Think of how many of these fourteen tasks are part of a mother's daily duties. Cooking dinner for our families is more than a chore (as it feels in my case) or a culinary adventure (as it is for some others); it's a work of mercy! Snapping a baby's onesie is clothing the naked, disciplining our sons and daughters is admonishing sinners, and praying that our children will be happy, healthy, and holy is a spir-itual work of mercy in itself. What a blessing that in the midst of our busy lives we can carry out these noble works without even leaving the house.

Just as we are called to care for the bodies and souls of our chil-dren in these ways, the Church is busy doing the same for her children. Consider the countless religious orders that have been founded for the sake of serving the physical needs of the poor. The hospitals and shelters run by Franciscans and Missionaries of Charity and the Little Sisters of the Poor come to mind, among so many others.

The charisms of other religious orders are directed more on the spiritual level, toward education, instruction, and prayer. Think, for example, of all the high schools and colleges established by the Jesuits. Or consider the Order of Preachers who, following in the footsteps of St. Dominic, bring the Gospel to life at the pulpit, calling us to conversion and repentance. Meanwhile, the cloistered Carmelite sisters pray for the living and the dead in the silence of their cells.

But, of course, the saints of the Church are not just members of religious orders. Recall all the work of countless lay Catholic associations, filled with husbands and wives, mothers and fathers, and single men and women who give of their "spare" time to establish or volunteer at soup kitchens, crisis pregnancy centers, Catholic counseling centers, and justice ministries for immigrants. Think of those laypeople who work in the diocesan offices that oversee social services, education, and prison outreach. The Church is busy at work making mercy manifest through all of these fruits of her family.

No one is to be excluded from receiving these benefits of the Church's service. She is called to welcome and accept anyone who comes to her in need, and to reach out in love to those who may not yet have the desire to approach her. As Pope Francis wrote on the eve of the Year of Mercy, "The Spouse of Christ must pattern her behaviour after the Son of God who went out to everyone without exception."[39]

Ultimately, this merciful outreach of the Church does more than meet people's basic needs. It also serves to remind everyone who receives this care that he or she is part of the Church's family. No one is forgotten. No one is too poor or too sinful to be welcomed into the fold.

The Church in her mercy embraces, among others, those women who at some point did not comprehend the dignity of their own motherhood or who were in such dire circumstances that they tragically chose to have an abortion. Mother Church does not abandon these daughters, who are so often the victims of abandonment or coercion from people who should have supported them. Instead, she offers forgiveness and mercy to all those who seek to return to her embrace.

This includes convicted criminals. They too should not be out of reach. Pope Francis emphasizes:

> Mother Church teaches us to be close to those who are in prison. "But no Father, this is dangerous, those are bad people." But each of us is capable…. Listen carefully to this: each of us is capable of doing the same thing that that man or that woman in prison did. All of us have the capacity to sin and to do the same, to make mistakes in life.[40]

This honest, humble recognition leads us to embrace everyone without condemnation. And such a warm welcome rejuvenates the one who receives it. Continuing his message about ministering to prisoners, the Holy Father says, "Mercy overcomes every wall, every barrier, and leads you to always seek the face of the man, of the person. And it is mercy which changes the heart and the life, which can regenerate a person and allow him or her to integrate into society in a new way."[41]

Not only do the Church's ministries help restore many to society; these acts of outreach also serve to remind her children that they have a home. They are part of a family. Pope Francis wrote of the Church:

> Her language and her gestures must transmit mercy, so as to touch the hearts of all people and inspire them once more to

find the road that leads to the Father...wherever the Church is present, the mercy of the Father must be evident. In our parishes, communities, associations and movements, in a word, wherever there are Christians, everyone should find an oasis of mercy.[42]

The Church is a mother who, like so many earthly mothers, longs to see her children gathered together at home, rejoicing in the loving embrace of their Father.

Another Mother's Voice: Linda's Story
Linda is the mother of three sons and two daughters and the grandmother of seventeen.

It was my mother who introduced me to Mother Church. As I was growing up, her faith shaped my world. We were there almost every time the church doors opened. Evenings of novenas to Our Lady of Perpetual Help, holy days, feast days—there were many occasions for coming to church.

Pushing open the huge doors of the church, I was enfolded by the smells, the beauty, the quiet. I followed my mother to a pew, kneeling, taking out my rosary, waiting for the prayers to begin. My mother, with her well-worn prayer books and her rosary, taught me that this mother, the Church, was always there waiting to enfold us, guide us, and love us.

As a young girl, my relationship with my mother hit a rough patch. I decided I wanted my friend's mother. I liked the things she did, the way she dressed, the fun outings she'd take us on. I could no longer see anything good in my mother, and I made life miserable for both of us. My mother loved me, but I wouldn't allow myself to receive that love. Yet, my mother continued to love me and reach out to me even when I turned away from that outstretched arm.

When I became a mother I started to "see," and the course of our relationship changed. I gained a new perspective because of my own daughter's rejection of me, our home, our life, and our values. I was devastated. I loved her intensely, but our relationship only got worse. But over time, God brought healing to my relationships. Now I absolutely delight in my daughter—and my mother has become my confidant, my prayer warrior, my friend, and one of the biggest blessings of my life.

As I look back, I can see how, just as I rejected my own mother at one time in my life, I experienced a similar time of "distancing" with Mother Church. As I entered adulthood, my love for God grew, but I began to separate this love from Mother Church. More and more of my friends were leaving the Church to attend other churches filled with musical praise, Scripture, small-group gatherings, active youth ministries, Sunday school, and so many delightful choices. I wanted out of the Catholic Church. My husband said no.

Because my husband refused to leave, I was "forced" to stay "home" with my mother the Catholic Church. So I cried out to God, "If there is anything here of value worth staying for, you will need to show me." God loves to take on that challenge. Thus began my rediscovery of the Catholic Church.

I had grown up with regular devotions to Mother Mary, but when I wanted to leave the Catholic Church, I felt I no longer needed Mary. For many years I wanted nothing to do with her. I would acknowledge she was the Mother of God and a great example for women, but even though the Church loved her and encouraged us to go to her for help and intercession, I didn't.

By the grace of God, it was my daughter who had once been separated from me that helped end my separation from Mother Mary. She purchased some Catholic CDs a few years ago and lent them to me. When I listened to *True Devotion*, by Father Lance Harlow, I began to understand God's plan for the Blessed Mother. My narrow, shallow understanding began to deepen and grow. I have since made a consecration to Our Lady. I am aware of Mother Mary throughout my day, guiding me through both the joys and sorrows of being a mother and grandmother, always leading me to her Son, Jesus.

And just as I began to grow in my understanding of Mary, I grew in my relationship with the Church as my mother, coming to see her also as a gift that is unsurpassed. I think of the riches of the banquet set before us—the Eucharist—the very presence of God given to transform me into the person he created me to be. I think of the Word of God, with its riches shared daily in the readings of the Mass, and of the Magisterium that Mother Church has set up for her children so that Scripture has protection from error. I think of the saints, my brothers and sisters, whose lives are there for me to learn from. I also think of the Blessed Mother. She is the Mother that the Church gives to each one of us.

- What elements of Linda's story resonate with your own? What touched, surprised, or inspired you about her reflection?

- Take a few moments to ponder or journal about how you have experienced the Church's motherly "acceptance" in your life. Then, turn to the study guide on page 116 for further reflection from the lives of the saints, the teaching of the Church, the liturgy, and the sacraments.

CHAPTER FIVE ··· Mothers Sacrifice

My mother-in-law gave birth to her children over a span of four decades. She started at the end of the fifties with her first child, and ended with her eleventh child in the beginning of the eighties. Including pregnancy, this means that she dedicated twenty-three years of her life to childbearing. I can hardly imagine a more excellent example of embracing the heroic sacrifices of maternity. To offer up this much of one's life to the trials of pregnancy, the pain of labor, and the demands of caring for infants—not to mention all the ensuing decades of nurturing a family—is a remarkable accomplishment.

For quite some time, I held the silent suspicion that somehow my mother-in-law was immune to all of these maternal challenges. I imagined her milking the cows at nine months pregnant with the same cheerful twinkle that graces her face today. I pictured her delivering each of her eleven children with the same unruffled endurance that she displays when I see her doing physical work in the house or garden. I supposed that she defeated the effects of prolonged sleep deprivation simply by the stoic calm with which she approaches all of the inevitable challenges of life.

Then I learned something shocking.

Immediately after the labor and delivery of her first child, my mother-in-law had declared to her husband, "I'm never doing that again."

Fifty years and ten children later, she revealed this story to my husband with a reminiscent chuckle. I was flabbergasted when Joe came home with the tale. "You mean *your* mother didn't like labor? *Your* mom thought it was going to be one and done?" This was a breakthrough moment for me in two ways.

First, I felt much better about my own maternal suffering. I suddenly felt like maybe I was not, in fact, the weakling I had imagined myself to be. If someone as strong and resilient as my mother-in-law could be overwhelmed by giving birth, then it didn't seem so bad for me to feel the same way. Perhaps motherhood really *is* objectively hard work.

Second, in that moment I realized what a hero Joe's mom truly is. It's easy to dismiss the sacrifices made by the mother of a large family when you imagine her floating through the experience on a golden cloud of bliss. But when it dawned on me that she had eleven children *even though it hurt*, I was brought to tears. Her sacrifices, the willingness to give of herself, the physical generosity that endured pregnancy and labor and midnight feedings for twenty-three years—all of this produced so much tangible good. It produced my husband, for one thing! And it produced ten other amazing people who walk the earth because their mother laid down her life for them.

White martyrdom, I've heard it called. It's a kind of death to self, the carrying of a cross that doesn't lead to the actual physical death of *red* martyrdom. I'm convinced that this kind of "dry" martyrdom is at the core of motherhood. And physical childbearing is not the only way it happens.

Adoptive mothers, for example, do not give birth to their children. Their white martyrdom is in the giving of themselves by serving their families, offering up physical and emotional energy to care for loved ones over the course of days, weeks, months, years, and decades, often while enduring silently the pain of being told that their children's "real" mother is someone else.

Many other women also care for children God places in their lives: stepmothers, godmothers, and (sometimes honorary) aunts who go the extra mile, and custodial grandmothers who care for extended family members in their own homes. All these dedicated women share in a kind of sacrificial maternal martyrdom in this way.

Think too of the sacrifices of single mothers who endure the tremendous emotional and social trials of unwed pregnancy for the sake of their child's life, and who continue to make extraordinary sacrifices of time and energy in order to provide for their family. Young widows who find themselves parenting alone also share in these extra sacrifices that join them to the ranks of the white martyrs. The same holds true for women who become single moms following the tragedy of separation, divorce, or abandonment.

There is also a kind of martyrdom for mothers of suffering children. I think of Mary standing at the foot of her Son's cross. Although she was not the one who died, undoubtedly she endured a kind of death in that terrible hour. I think about what might have been going through her heart and her head at that most horrible of moments. Simeon's prophetic message from her Son's infancy, "And a sword will pierce your own soul too" (Luke 2:35), must have come true at the foot of the cross. Witnessing the brutal torture of her beloved boy who was "wounded for our transgressions" (Isaiah 53:5) at the hands of hateful men had to feel like being mortally wounded herself. Frankly, I can't imagine the pain. But I'm sure some mothers can.

Mothers who have accompanied their children through illness and death, no doubt, have a personal insight into this kind of pain. I recall the words of my grandmother who cared for her suffering daughter and sat by her bedside as she died of breast cancer at thirty-eight years old. Grandma told me years later that a mother should never have to live to attend the funeral of one of her own children.

Mothers who have lost their sons or daughters because of war, religious persecution, or martyrdom can undoubtedly also relate to feeling their hearts pierced through. Lest we imagine that no such mothers exist in today's world, let us remember that Christian persecution and *red* martyrdom is a tragic reality in many parts of the world right now. Every victim is someone's child.

Women who have suffered miscarriage, stillbirth, or infant death also know the piercing pain of losing a child. These mothers have given of themselves, even for children so very young. Indeed, the martyrdom of mothers begins with gestation. Even if a pregnancy does not come to full term, the expectant mother makes sacrifices for her child from the beginning.

When an unborn child takes up residence in his mother's womb, he necessarily makes a host of demands upon her body, her energy, and even her emotions. The range and intensity of symptoms varies from woman to woman, but whether pregnancy involves nausea, high blood pressure, indigestion, fatigue, or depression, the mother literally "knits" a new human person out of the store of her own physical resources. So, too, her body becomes a home for this growing child, so that even if she is blissfully spared the early discomforts of pregnancy, she will not be spared the late ones as her waist expands and her feet grow further and further out of reach.

Then comes childbirth. This is the pinnacle of the physical self-gift of the mother. Again, the level of intensity is diverse, but the principle is the same for every woman. She literally lays down her life, offering up her body and her blood to give life to her child. For many women, this feat of physical strength is also accompanied by a great deal of fear, particularly for first-time moms.

When I was nearing the fulfillment of my first pregnancy, my parish priest asked how I was doing. I told him I felt like I was experiencing a kind of agony in the garden. I knew what lay ahead—childbirth—and prayed to God that it wouldn't end in my own death. I was afraid that I would die giving birth.

It was much less traumatic to approach labor the second time, confident that I had already navigated it successfully! But every woman who has tried to breathe through contractions while under an oxygen mask, or witnessed the nervous strain of an obstetrician who's trying not to let on, or who has endured the drama of an emergency C-section knows how nearly childbirth can approach red martyrdom.

Thankfully, as most mothers will attest, it's all worth it. I love the fact that our Lord spoke about this. Jesus understood well our maternal trials, but he also understood the great joy that follows. "When a woman is in labor, she has pain, because her hour has come. But when her child is born, she no longer remembers the anguish because of the joy of having brought a human being into the world" (John 16:21).

When a mother gives birth to a child, she uniquely imitates Christ in how she mirrors the paschal mystery: through the pains of labor and the resulting gift of newborn life, she enters into the sacrifice of Christ, taking up her cross and following him all the way to resurrection.

St. Paul wrote that women "will be saved through childbearing" (1 Timothy 2:15). I suspect that bearing a child in one's body has a salvific character because the experience leads us into the redemptive mystery of the cross. Every mother who delivers a child offers her body and sheds her blood to give life, just as Christ did on the cross. And at every Mass, Mother Church continues to offer this sacrifice of Christ's Body and Blood in union with the faithful.

Mother Church Sacrifices

Every once in a while, a priest celebrating Mass will lose his place in the book of prayers during the Eucharistic consecration. While he pauses to regain his bearings, I usually find myself continuing the prayers in my head anyway. The words are so very familiar. "Take this, all of you, and eat of it. For this is my Body, which will be given up for you."[43] Then, similarly, "Take this, all of you, and drink from it, for this is the chalice of my Blood, the Blood of the new and eternal covenant, which will be poured out for you and for many for the forgiveness of sins."[44]

Regular churchgoers hear these words at least once a week. They make up part of the "soundtrack" of our Catholic faith. But it's important to realize that even though the priest is ordained to stand *in persona Christi* and say these words, he is not the only one involved in the offering.

In the celebration of Mass, through the ministry of the priest, the Church participates in making the Eucharistic sacrifice to God the Father. And *we* are part of the Church. This is not just the action of Christ or the action of the celebrating minister. It is our action, too. The *Catechism* tells us:

> *The Eucharist is also the sacrifice of the Church.* The Church which is the Body of Christ participates in the offering of her Head. With him, she herself is offered whole and entire.... In the Eucharist the sacrifice of Christ becomes also the sacrifice of the members of his Body. (CCC, 1368)

We, of course, are these members! As such, through the Eucharist our lives are united to Christ and his offering. The sacrifice of Christ made present on the altar enables all Christians to join themselves to his offering.[45]

So, each one of us helps Mother Church to make her sacrifice. We jointly offer our praise, our sufferings, our prayers, and our work together as a community of faith. And through the sacramental mystery, these little offerings of ours are joined to the one supreme offering of Jesus: his death on the cross. The *Catechism* teaches, "The sacrifice of Christ and the sacrifice of the Eucharist are *one single sacrifice*" (CCC, 1367).

The gift and privilege of participating in the Eucharistic sacrifice ought to have a special meaning to mothers. We can bring to the altar the wide array of sufferings and sacrifices that we endure in the course of our vocation. We join with Mother Church when we gather at Mass, and lay before the Father our maternal sufferings: all the sleepless nights, all the anxiety over our children's welfare, the discomforts of childbearing and child-rearing, the sorrows of family discord, and every other challenge we face. We also offer here the sacrifice of our work—the laundry, the cooking, the cleaning, the organizing, the bill paying, or whatever other vast array of daily duties we undertake.

But we bring to the altar also our praise. Mother Church encourages us to remember our blessings even as we lay down our burdens. So we come to Mass to praise God for our families, our marriages, and our children's lives, for the joys they bring and the gifts they offer to us and to the world. How beautiful that God invites us to make a "sacrifice of praise."

Of course, it is always easier to offer praise to God when things are going well. But surely the most powerful sacrifice of praise is one that is made even in the midst of trial. So, when we bring our burdens before the Lord but still praise him nonetheless—even for the ways these burdens make us stronger—then our sacrifice becomes all the more powerful.

Mother Church gives us an example of how to praise God even in the midst of tremendous suffering every time she commemorates the life of a martyr. In the martyrs, we tangibly encounter the tragedy of the persecuted Church. We see innocence, virtue, and faith brutally punished in the way the courageous martyrs were treated.

Yet, the Church does not give in to despair. She does not allow the sorrow of these situations to overcome her. Instead, she offers a *sacrifice of praise.* She thanks God for the strength and the witness of her persecuted children. She holds them up as examples to inspire her other children. And she rejoices in the merits that those faithful sons and daughters won through their suffering.

Thus, the Church has special prayers and masses in honor of the martyrs. She offers the Eucharist on the feast days of these holy men and women, specifically recalling what they endured and joining it to the sacrifice of Christ. One such prayer from the Common of Martyrs says, "In honor of the precious death of your just ones, O Lord, we come to offer that sacrifice from which all martyrdom draws its origin."[46]

Indeed, Christian martyrdom has its origin in the sacrifice of Christ on the cross. (Thus, unlike violent and suicidal religious "martyrdom," a Christian martyr never intends others to suffer, but rather suffers *at the hands* of others). The strength these courageous witnesses have demonstrated in dying for the Lord comes from their willingness to be united to his sufferings. And although the sufferings they undergo will always remain a tragedy, God has a way of transforming death into new life. Thus, the example of these brave Christians serves to strengthen and fortify the Church. "The blood of the martyrs is the seed of the Church,"[47] wrote Tertullian in the late second century. The sacrifice of their lives is not meaningless, but becomes a powerful testimony to the strength of Christian conviction.

Many of us are familiar with the names of virgin martyrs like St. Lucia, St. Agnes, and St. Agatha, who suffered during the Roman persecutions of the first centuries AD. But that era also saw martyrs who were mothers, like Sts. Perpetua and Felicity. Perpetua was a young noblewoman, and a nursing mother, when she was arrested because of her Christian faith. Felicity was a slave who was eight months pregnant when she joined Perpetua in prison.

Two days before their scheduled execution, Felicity gave birth to her daughter. As Felicity was in labor, the guards mocked her, saying, "If you're complaining now, what will you do when you'll be thrown to the wild beasts?"[48] Felicity's answer reveals that she understood, on the eve of her martyrdom, that God would give her the strength she needed. She calmly told the cruel guards, "Now it is I who suffer, but then another shall be in me to bear the pain for me."[49]

The early Christians were not the only ones who died for their faith, however. Many other eras have seen (and continue to see) the persecution of Christians. I think of another mother martyr, St. Margaret Clitherow, who suffered during the sixteenth-century persecutions associated with King Henry VIII's English Reformation.

A convert to Catholicism and the mother of three children, Margaret bravely assisted fugitive Catholic priests, hiding them in her home and inviting them to celebrate Mass there secretly. Her "crime" was discovered, and she was arrested. But Margaret refused to go to trial because her children would have been called in to testify and most likely would have suffered torture. Therefore, for the sake of her faith and her children's well-being, she endured the sentence of being crushed to death on Good Friday 1586.

Lest we imagine that such dramatic stories are merely from the past, it's important to be aware that the witness of persecuted Christians continues today, particularly in the Middle East. Some of us recall news reports about a kind of modern Felicity, Meriam Ibrahim, a Sudanese Christian who was eight months pregnant when she was imprisoned with her twenty-month-old son. She had been sentenced to death for apostasy in June 2014 because she married a Christian man. Thanks to the influence of the international community, however, she was released after eighteen months in jail.

Perhaps not as many of us heard the story of two eighty-year-old Iraqi women, Victoria and Gazella, who were left behind in their village, which most people had evacuated as the Islamic extremists of Daesh (ISIS) approached. Aid to the Church in Need—a Catholic charity under the guidance of the Holy Father—commissioned a study called *Persecuted and Forgotten? A Report on Christians Oppressed for Their Faith 2013–2015*. The report tells of the courage of these two elderly Christian women:

> After four days, they were discovered by the militants who frog marched them to St Barbara's Hill on the edge of the village where they joined 10 other Christians. When they were ordered to convert to Islam, Victoria and Gazella refused. Gazella said: "We believe that if we show love and kindness, forgiveness and mercy we can bring about the kingdom of God on earth as well as in heaven. Paradise is about love. If you want to kill us for our faith then we are prepared to die here and now." Daesh had no response to the women's resolute faith and it was agreed that the remaining dozen or so Christians could go free.[50]

The stories of all of these women, along with countless others, give us concrete examples of the suffering Church. The concept is not meant to be an abstraction. The sacrifices of Mother Church through her persecuted children are as tangible as Gazella standing on that hill in Iraq. But the Church offers sacrifices in still another way.

Whenever a member of the body of Christ suffers, that suffering can be offered up as a sacrifice in union with the suffering of Christ for the benefit of the whole Church. When we practice the traditional Catholic spirituality of offering up our sufferings—be they great or small—we transform them into sacrifices on behalf of the Church. This practice is based in Scripture. St. Paul writes, "I am now rejoicing in my sufferings for your sake, and in my flesh I am completing what is lacking in Christ's afflictions for the sake of his body, that is, the church" (Colossians 1:24). Paul—a member of the Church—offers his sufferings for the sake of the Church. And many other saints throughout history have also offered their sufferings in this way.

The sacrifices made by the holy men and women who have gone before us can actually benefit *us*. Traditional language refers to these benefits as the merits of the saints. Through their lives of virtue, and through the challenges they endured with heroic faith, the saints have helped to build up a store of goodness that can be shared with anyone in need. Pope Francis writes:

> The Church lives within the communion of the saints. In the Eucharist, this communion, which is a gift from God, becomes a spiritual union binding us to the saints and blessed ones whose number is beyond counting (cf. Revelation 7:4). Their holiness comes to the aid of our weakness in a way that enables the Church, with her maternal prayers and her way of life, to fortify the weakness of some with the strength of others.[51]

The concept of these shared merits is a bit foreign to our modern sensibilities, but it's not all that different than the idea of praying for someone. We believe that you and I can offer a prayer for someone who doesn't have the wherewithal to pray for herself. I can ask God to help her, to comfort or convert her. And God in his infinite wisdom and power can use my prayer for her benefit if he so chooses. It's an experience of communal support that happens on an invisible, spiritual level.

The treasure trove of saintly merit is similar. God can spread all of this superabundant goodness wherever he wants to, and it just so happens that he uses the Church to help him do some of the spreading. Through his Son, the Father has given Mother Church the power to "bind and loose" (see Matthew 18:18). She thus has the authority to call upon the merits of her children and share them as she sees fit.

Don't we see something like this happening with our children from time to time? One of my daughters loves to help in the kitchen. When she comes up with a new recipe, we all benefit by eating the (usually) tasty creations. Another daughter is a fabulous reader, and the younger kids benefit from this gift because they get to sit next to her and hear their favorite stories when Mom is too busy to read. My son loves to engineer inventions, and from time to time he comes up with something that actually makes a task or chore easier for all of us. We share our gifts. The talents of one make up for the deficiencies of another. It's what families do.

And the saints are part of our Catholic family. So when the wife, doctor, and mother of four, St. Gianna Beretta Molla, heroically offered her life to save her unborn daughter in 1962, her generosity and courage became part of the merits of the saints.

When Venerable Conchita Cabrera de Armida—a mother of nine who was widowed when her youngest was two—died at the age of sixty-five in 1937, she left behind more than her family. She had also established a spiritual apostolate called "Works of the Cross" in Mexico. But her sanctity was won primarily through devotion to her maternal vocation. "Saint or mystic we do not know," her children reported, "but mother, the greatest mother that ever lived!"[52] This courageous mother also contributed to the merits of the saints.

When Chiara Corbella Petrillo endured the loss of two babies without bitterness, she transformed tragedy into a sacrifice of praise. Twice she gave birth to children with abnormalities, whom doctors had wanted to abort. And twice she watched her infants die in her arms within minutes of birth, but gave thanks to God nonetheless for the gift of their lives.

Continuing to welcome life in spite of these losses, Chiara gave birth to a healthy third child later on, having postponed treatment for cancer to save her unborn baby. The cancer finally claimed her life in 2012 when she was twenty-eight years old. In the face of all her suffering, however, those who knew Chiara remember her as a witness to joy. Even though she's not formally canonized, Chiara's life of virtue is a gift to the whole Church.

We need not be formally declared saints to offer such gifts. We too are invited to make these offerings of our lives and our sufferings for the sake of our family of faith. Indeed, all this sacrificial work of the Church is not just for someone else, somewhere else. The Second Vatican Council referred to the Church as the People of God and emphasized that we—the people—are all called to holiness.[53]

This brings us to an important point about Mother Church that Pope Francis has made:

> The Church is not distinct from us, but should be seen as the totality of believers, as the "we" of Christians: I, you, we all are part of the Church.... Thus the motherhood of the Church is lived by us all, pastors and faithful.... We all take part in the motherhood of the church, so that the light of Christ may reach the far confines of the earth.[54]

Of course, one of the most literal ways to take the light of Christ to the ends of the earth is through missionary activity. This is yet another way that Mother Church offers sacrifice. Think of all the missionaries throughout the history of the Church who have given up home, family, friends, and countless comforts to travel to distant lands for the sake of the Gospel. And think of the mothers who have watched their sons and daughters embark upon such frightful missions!

St. Isaac Jogues was a French Jesuit priest who left his home to evangelize the Iroquois, Huron, and other native populations living in the New World in the early seventeenth century. His mother had tried to persuade him to minister at home in France, but Isaac was resolute. In a letter to Madame Jogues that he composed after his arrival near Quebec, Isaac wrote:

Every year, with the grace of God, you will receive a letter from me and I shall await letters from you, also, once a year. Please forward these to Paris in the beginning of March.... It will always be a consolation to receive news of you and of our family, for I have no hope ever to see you again in this life. May God in His Goodness unite us all in His holy abode, where we may praise Him through all eternity.[55]

This is what it once meant to send your son off as a missionary! In today's era of Skype and e-mail and Boeing 747s, we can hardly imagine such minimal contact with a beloved child. But sacrifices of this degree have been made by countless Christian families throughout the centuries for the sake of helping Mother Church to reach her children even in the remotest parts of the earth.

Another Mother's Voice: Becky's Story

Becky is the mother of three sons, one daughter,
and one baby on the way.

It's hard to reflect upon motherhood when you're battling morning sickness. It's like trying to describe a beautiful sunset when you're caught in a hailstorm without an umbrella. But it is the very nature of motherhood—full of its sacrifices and messiness—that in fact makes it *beautiful*. So in that regard, it's quite fitting that I tap my maternal muse in between bouts of nausea and panic attacks over how I'm going to handle a household of five kids ten and under.

I admit that I wasn't always the first person to applaud motherhood. I was a self-proclaimed feminist who hummed the anthem of women's lib, which of course included a special homage to the so-called empowerment of contraception and a woman's "right" to abortion as part of her freedom and choice. I don't know why I didn't make the connection at the time that we can't speak of celebrating womanhood when everything we promote seeks to unplug or mutilate the very essence of what makes us *women*.

It wasn't that I didn't want children someday. I just saw the whole project as beneath my full "potential." In fact, when my dad once mentioned that my mom always dreamed of being an actress and a mommy, I scoffed, feeling those goals were rather paltry. Many years later I would recognize the ironic fact that it was her very dream that allowed me to stand in judgment of it.

It wasn't until I became acquainted with the Catholic Church and more specifically Pope St. John Paul II's Theology of the Body that I discovered the deeper reality of feminine dignity, especially in its inherent connection to the maternal call of all women. Our culture taught me to reject or exploit my feminine nature. The Catholic Church is the only entity that taught me to embrace it.

Not surprisingly, the Church's teaching on women, motherhood, life, and marriage as an icon of Trinitarian love became the antidote to my poisoned understanding of womanhood. Still, seven months into my first pregnancy, I was worried that I was created without a maternal instinct.

And then my midwife handed me my son.

The truth I knew in my heart became personal—just like God became personal when he stepped into our humanity.

The more I loved, the more I wanted to love. And my spiritual antenna became more attuned to the frequency of the Holy Spirit. It's how I knew we were called to be open to a second unique, unrepeatable soul far sooner than we had originally intended, and how I've continued to sense when we're missing someone before he or she is even conceived. Where once I feared the conception of new life inside my body, I now welcome it. Where once I was afraid of large families, I am more open to having a fifth than I was a third.

The maternal instinct I always thought was lacking was actually stifled by my rejection of the Church and her truth. Once I accepted her, I came to know myself. Because the Church herself is feminine, there is a natural parallel between her mission and mine. An open embrace to all, she is also a shelter to the most sacred—the life of the Spirit, the life of the faithful, and of course the most significant, a womb in which Christ himself resides.

I return to this thought often when I'm throwing up, battling a two-year-old's meltdowns, cleaning up a four-year-old's potty accidents, and combatting a seven-year-old's back talk or a nine-year-old's laziness. My being, my home, my motherhood, is a conduit through which Christ reveals, transforms, and perfects from within. And I get to participate, despite my imperfection!

I realized my feminine design, expanding and contracting through each pregnancy, is literally part of humanity's heartbeat—a feminine pulse that pumps life and love into God's creation. As woman, I reflect Mary's fiat every time I become a vessel of incarnated love between me and my husband.

As mother, I get to reflect Christ's authentic love through my own personhood. I have now five times said, "This is my body, given up for you." I have endured the great suffering of childbirth, literally shedding both blood and water for new life, emptying myself so that I become more of who I am meant to be. And I am, daily, stretched and pruned as I unconditionally love, nurture, discipline, guide, and educate these precious creatures who drive me crazy— just like the Church does for her faithful.

This is my maternal call, which I found only when I answered the Catholic Church's maternal call to me.

- What elements of Becky's story resonate with your own? What touched, surprised, or inspired you about her reflection?

- Take a few moments to ponder or journal about how you have experienced the Church's motherly "sacrifice" in your life. Then, turn to the study guide on page 118 for further reflection from the lives of the saints, the teaching of the Church, the liturgy, and the sacraments.

CHAPTER SIX ··· Mothers Heal

My three-year-old son was blowing out the candles on his birthday cake when the hemorrhage began. I was eight weeks pregnant with our fourth child, and I instantly knew there was a problem. Not wanting to put a damper on the birthday celebration, I slipped upstairs and assessed the situation. Based on the amount of bleeding I saw, it seemed extremely unlikely that the baby was still alive. I laid down on my bed and tried to stay calm as the chills set in.

Within five minutes, my mother was right next to me. She had noticed my disappearance and came to check on me. She wrapped me in blankets and brought me a cup of tea. Soon enough, *her* mother came upstairs and joined us. My grandma is an awesome prayer warrior. I told her what was happening, and she immediately found some holy water, laid her hands on me, and began praying. She pleaded to God to save the life of my baby.

The bleeding continued, and so my doctor set up an ultrasound for the next day. Joe and I went to the appointment expecting the worst. We had been through one early miscarriage already and prepped ourselves for a similar emotional experience. But as we glanced hesitantly at the monitor, we rejoiced to see a beating heart. The image showed that our prayers were answered, and the baby was still alive and well. However, the image also showed the ominous presence of a subchorionic hemorrhage. The doctor informed us that either this pool of misplaced blood would grow and grow until it caused the miscarriage of a perfectly healthy baby, or it would shrink and shrink until it disappeared.

We began praying again, along with many family members and friends, that the hemorrhage would disappear. Meanwhile, I was put on partial bed rest. With three children four and under, this was a tough assignment. But my mother arranged to stay with us indefinitely (my parents had been visiting from out of town for the birthday party) in order to lend a hand. She helped to "mother" my children for the next six weeks, feeding, dressing, entertaining, and caring for them while I tried to move as little as possible.

How grateful I was for my mother during those weeks. Not only did she help me to maintain bed rest; she also comforted me tremendously as I struggled through the nausea and malaise of my first trimester. My mom had not planned to be away from my dad or her home for so long. Her schedule had not included spending a month and a half caring for the daily needs of a crew of young children and tending to a sick daughter. But she accepted this situation with incredible grace.

In addition to all the physical assistance she gave our family, she also offered me precious emotional assistance. I was struggling with anxiety and depression from the hormones of pregnancy topped by my concern about the fate of my baby, but my mother was a source of strength. She encouraged me, cheered me up when I needed it, and brought me inspirational readings to lift my spirits. She kept a positive attitude and looked on the bright side, but without dismissing my concerns. She listened with compassion, all the while continuing to keep my mug full of the ginger tea that eased my nausea.

And she eased my spirit, too. I questioned why God had allowed this situation to happen in the first place, on top of everything else. This was a time of spiritual trial for me—as well as physical and emotional—but all the while my mother was at my side, reminding me to put my trust in God. She prayed with me, and she prayed for me, and if she ever doubted God's will, she didn't let on. Instead, she was like a rock of faith during those terribly trying times.

Finally, after what seemed an eternity, the time came to have another ultrasound. Thanks be to God, the hemorrhage had completely disappeared without a trace. The baby was growing well, and we rejoiced. God had answered our prayers again, and we were truly grateful.

Six months later, our baby girl was born weighing in at a robust nine pounds, ten ounces, and measuring twenty-one inches long. I could not help but think that her survival was connected to my mother's generous, loving service. If I hadn't been able to stay off my feet, chances are that the hemorrhage would have been aggravated and the outcome might have been different.

My mother's presence among us for those weeks was truly a healing one. Not only did she help me persevere through the real trials of my not-just-in-the-morning sickness, but she was also a healing agent in the recovery of my body. She helped me defeat that hemorrhage. Without a doubt, her mothering contributed to the victory over that physical threat.

While this is perhaps the most dramatic episode of my mother's healing presence, she has had the same general effect throughout the course of my life. Although I have never suffered from a serious illness, I have plenty of memories of my mom caring for me when I was sick. Her compassion for me and my brothers whenever we were suffering, physically or otherwise, was always easy to see and feel. When I was home from school with the flu, for example, she would ease the misery of the experience by setting up a little station for me. A can of 7-Up with a bendy straw, some tissues, a few saltines, and a book or the remote control would all sit atop a TV tray in the family room while I recuperated on the couch. But more than these items, her comforting presence always helped me feel better.

I remember being sick when I first moved away from home. It was emotionally disorienting. The flu itself felt worse than it ever had before because on top of the symptoms of the illness, I was missing the soothing presence of my mom. I was in this alone, and it was frightening. My mother had never magically cured me, but it was clear that she had always helped me to feel better.

Now, as I care for my children when they are sick, I think of the difference that my mother made. I try to be the same kind of compassionate companion for them, a calming presence that reassures them and takes away any fear. I set up my own version of the sickness station when necessary, and respond to their needs with as much patience and love as I can muster. I can't say for sure that the children experience it the way I did, but I suspect that my presence in these moments is a healing one for them, too.

Mother Church Heals

Is the Church a healing presence in our lives? She should be. This is part of her nature. The *Catechism* tells us:

> The Lord Jesus Christ, physician of our souls and bodies, who forgave the sins of the paralytic and restored him to bodily health, has willed that his Church continue, in the power of the Holy Spirit, his work of healing and salvation, even among her own members. (CCC, 1421)

The Church continues to do what Jesus did to safeguard and restore people's spiritual and physical health. The example of the healing of the paralytic is a helpful one to illustrate the relationship between these two elements. In the story, Jesus shows his concern for the man's physical health in addition to his spiritual well-being:

> Then some people came, bringing to him a paralyzed man, carried by four of them. And when they could not bring him to Jesus because of the crowd, they removed the roof above him; and after having dug through it, they let down the mat on which the paralytic lay. When Jesus saw their faith, he said to the paralytic, "Son, your sins are forgiven." Now some of the scribes were sitting there, questioning in their hearts, "Why does this fellow speak in this way? It is

blasphemy! Who can forgive sins but God alone?" At once Jesus perceived in his spirit that they were discussing these questions among themselves; and he said to them, "Why do you raise such questions in your hearts? Which is easier, to say to the paralytic, 'Your sins are forgiven,' or to say, 'Stand up and take your mat and walk'? But so that you may know that the Son of Man has authority on earth to forgive sins"— he said to the paralytic—"I say to you, stand up, take your mat and go to your home." And he stood up, and immediately took the mat and went out before all of them; so that they were all amazed and glorified God, saying, "We have never seen anything like this!" (Mark 2:3–12)

Why did Jesus begin by forgiving the man's sins? Doesn't it seem that his friends went to the trouble of carrying the paralytic man so that Jesus would heal his *body*? How does the forgiveness of sins relate to the restoration of full health?

Because we are human beings made of both body and soul, our fullest "recovery" involves both elements of ourselves. Even if we are physically intact, we are still lacking something if our souls are afflicted by the wounds of sin. And many would argue that what we lack in such a case is not just on the spiritual level, but that our bodies are also negatively affected when our souls are suffering. Being in right relationship with God brings a kind of peace with it. This can in turn help the body to function better.

Medical research has offered scientific evidence to this effect. One study indicated that religious patients "reported significantly lower levels of pain, even though they were no less likely to report the presence of pain."[56] Our health is more than just a physical reality. It has a spiritual element as well. The *Catechism* clarifies this for us in relation to Jesus's ministry of healing:

Jesus has the power not only to heal, but also to forgive sins; he has come to heal the whole man, soul and body; he is the physician the sick have need of. His compassion toward all who suffer goes so far that he identifies himself with them: "I was sick and you visited me." (CCC, 1503)

Jesus certainly spent much of his ministry curing people's physical ailments, but his mission was broader than this. Mark's Gospel records a moment when Jesus spoke clearly on the subject: "Those who are well have no need of a physician, but those who are sick. Go and learn what this means, 'I desire mercy, not sacrifice.' For I have come to call not the righteous but sinners" (Matthew 9:12–13). Jesus understood that sinners were in need of a kind of healing, just like a sick person is in need of a doctor. And he understood that he came to earth to call sinners to himself, to call them to repentance, reconciliation, and restoration. He often issued this "call" in conjunction with physical healings. And as the *Catechism* teaches, through the sacraments, "Christ continues to 'touch' us in order to heal us" (CCC, 1504).

This healing is what Mother Church offers to her children. Specifically, through the sacraments of healing—reconciliation (also called the sacrament of penance or confession) and anointing of the sick—the Church helps to comfort us in our afflictions of soul and body.

The sacrament of reconciliation uses one of the most maternal methods of healing in existence: conversation. How often do children turn to their mothers for a listening ear? How many concerns and anxieties, frustrations and fears, have we laid upon our mothers' shoulders through our conversations over the years? How many of these things have we taken upon our shoulders as we have mothered our own children? A devoted mother is available to listen to her children, to speak with them, to hear them out, and of course to offer words of consolation, encouragement, and support. Even when she cannot "cure" the problem, her receptive presence nonetheless has a healing effect.

When we take part in the sacrament of reconciliation, we enjoy being in the presence of Mother Church and having all the benefits of her listening ear. How appropriate that we should be asked to speak to her! How appropriate that, through this sacrament, we have a human encounter with the priest, who listens to us and speaks to us on behalf of Christ and his Church. What a tangible, concrete way to receive the healing touch our souls long to experience.

After we share our stories and our struggles in this sacramental dialogue, the priest may offer us words of spiritual direction or advice. Or, at times, he may simply pray the words of absolution, which in themselves are healing words:

> God, the Father of mercies, through the death and the resurrection of his Son has reconciled the world to himself and sent the Holy Spirit among us for the forgiveness of sins; through the ministry of the Church may God give you pardon and peace, and I absolve you from your sins in the name of the Father, and of the Son, and of the Holy Spirit.[57]

How reassuring to hear with our own ears this prayer of forgiveness. How beautiful to know that the priest absolves us "through the ministry of the Church," our spiritual mother. The "pardon and peace" that comes from this sacrament is not just for our souls. Walking out of the confessional generally brings with it a sense of relief that permeates our entire body. It enables us to enjoy the feeling of having a weight lifted off of our shoulders. We walk in, burdened by our sins, but walk out feeling the freedom of forgiveness.

Like a good mother, the Church listens. But also, like a good mother, she directs us. Where she sees need for improvement or change, she tells us honestly and lovingly, offering concrete guidance for how to proceed. This is what happens through the "penance" element of the sacrament. The priest gives the penitent a kind of assignment, often involving prayer (saying the Lord's Prayer, for example) or sometimes involving action (such as, "Be sure to tell your husband you love him when you go home").

This penance is meant to help us in two ways. First, it helps us show our sorrow by trying to the best of our ability to do something that helps make up for the harm we caused. This is why penance is also called "satisfaction" or "reparation." But the penance is also meant to help us change. It is designed to assist us in overcoming the temptation to sin again, and to orient us toward doing what is right.

This is part of the teaching that a mother is called to do for her children. When one of my children hurts or offends a sibling or parent, I encourage them not only to say they are sorry, but to think of a "penance" that *shows* they are sorry and helps to make things right again. Doing something nice for the person they hurt, offering to share something special, or helping with a task are a few examples. Sometimes the strategy works better than others, but in general I find that these concrete actions are very helpful for restoring peace.

In addition to offering us the great sacrament of spiritual healing, the Church also comforts us through the sacrament of anointing of the sick. In the Epistle of St. James, we hear about this practice from the earliest days of the Church: "Are any among you sick? They should call for the elders of the church and have them pray over them, anointing them with oil in the name of the Lord" (James 5:14–15). This is just what a priest does in the sacrament. He lays his hands on the person who is ill, praying for healing of body and soul, and then anoints him or her with blessed oil.

This rite clearly encourages the warmth of human touch. The sacrament helps to satisfy our human need for a real physical encounter with one another in moments of trial. A mother's care for her sick child inevitably involves touching him or her. Here again, through the ministry of her priests, Mother Church reaches out to touch her children. As a result, those who participate in the sacrament receive "strengthening, peace and courage to overcome the difficulties that go with the condition of serious illness or the frailty of old age" (CCC, 1520).

Sometimes, the sacrament leads to physical recovery. Many of us have heard stories of miraculous healings that came upon reception of the last rites, as the anointing of the sick is often called. But regardless of a sudden cure, this sacrament does bring spiritual healing. The *Catechism* tells us that the anointing "is meant to lead the sick person to healing of the soul, but also of the body if such is God's will. Furthermore, 'if he has committed sins, he will be forgiven'" (CCC, 1520).

Although the spiritual repair work may not always lead to a physical *cure*, it does lead to a kind of physical healing. The peace that comes from the sacrament often has a calming effect on the body. I remember seeing this clearly when I was present at the hospital during my uncle's last hours. Although he was unconscious, his restless body had been flailing in distress for several days. He was restrained with straps that kept him from throwing himself off of the bed as he labored with heavy breathing and tossed and sweated. The high doses of pain meds could not seem to bring relief. Finally, a priest came in with his *Pastoral Care of the Sick* book and said the prayers. The response from my uncle was astonishing. His body relaxed, the distress ceased, and before the end of the day he passed away in peace.

My uncle had not been a practicing Catholic for many years. It was my grandmother's hope and prayer, however, that he would receive the last rites of the Church before he died. When his death seemed imminent, she got in the car and traveled over a thousand miles to be at his bedside. The visit of that local priest, a near miracle in itself, was the direct result of her fervent intercession.

She knew that morphine wasn't the solution. At that most significant hour, her son needed the healing touch of his spiritual mother, the Church.

Another Mother's Voice: Veronica's Story

Veronica is the mother of four daughters and two sons, the grandmother of twenty-three, and the great-grandmother of forty-five.

In my old age, I look back and I feel so blessed that I was raised by my parents in Holy Mother Church. I don't even want to think about what my life would have been without the Catholic Church.

My mother taught me how to pray. I remember she taught me the Our Father and the Hail Mary. I didn't see her praying very often, but I think she did it quietly. When things were stressful, though, we would all pray the rosary. I remember my mother getting us up at night to pray the rosary when my father was out drinking. Maybe those prayers kept him alive. I also remember her praying for my brother when he was overseas during World War II. That probably kept him alive, too.

Faith wasn't talked about much in our house, but my parents were very insistent on attending Mass on Sundays and holy days, and that wasn't always easy, since we lived on a farm that was far away from the church. My mother seemed to know about the Catholic Church. It was important to her. We probably would not have gone if it was up to my dad.

When it was time to get married, I just knew my future husband had to be Catholic. Lawrence felt the same about his future wife. Being Catholic was just taken for granted. I was in the Altar Society and went to meetings once a month. But when Lawrence attended a Cursillo retreat, our marriage really changed. The environment in our home changed. Lawrence was on fire for his faith, and it was so helpful to us as a couple.

I was a very dominating force in our home. The Cursillo movement helped me put my husband in a different role as the head of the home. That was an important lesson! But the Catholic Church was really in the lead.

Being a mother and a grandmother hasn't always been easy. But when anything comes up, I run to the Lord. I don't know how anyone lives without faith. I guess I should be grateful for my simple mind, because I'm totally dependent on God. Intellect can be a hindrance to dealing with suffering. I try to surrender everything to the Lord. Sometimes I just repeat 1 Thessalonians 5:18: "In all things give thanks." I have seen how powerful praise can be. It is hard to praise in so many situations, but praise works.

Lawrence battled leukemia for several years. When he was ill, we would pray over him. I remember when he had been so, so sick, and we were supposed to go on a trip to Ohio. I wanted to call a priest, but it took Lawrence a while to agree. Our pastor finally came and anointed him. The next day, Lawrence was well, and we were on the way to Ohio! We prayed for his complete healing, but prayers aren't always answered the way we want. But I always feel it's God's will. There is nothing that can happen to us that God cannot turn unto good.

Lawrence died in 1985. I've been a widow for thirty years. The older I get, the more alone I feel. But I don't feel so alone when I go to church. I am so grateful to God for the Holy Catholic Church, for the comforts I find there.

There are so many ways the Church has been ministering to me over these ninety-one years. The Church has mothered me through her priests, and through the sacraments. No other church has the power of the priest. Mother Church makes it possible for us to receive Jesus in Holy Communion. And the Holy Father has been ministering to me all these years. The Church gives us a pope to tell us what the Church is teaching. She is the oldest Church in the world, the one Jesus founded.

I don't know how to put it all in words. I read a quote from Caryll Houselander about the Catholic Church that I like. The Church is "the refuge and hope of all sinners, the joy and hope of all saints, the life and hope of every living creature."[58]

I can't really explain it. I just know I am dependent on Mother Church. It's built into my being. I can't imagine getting along without her. What a blessing to have such a godly, healing Mother!

- What elements of Veronica's story resonate with your own? What touched, surprised, or inspired you about her reflection?

- Take a few moments to ponder or journal about how you have experienced the Church's motherly "healing" in your life. Then, turn to the study guide on page 120 for further reflection from the lives of the saints, the teaching of the Church, the liturgy, and the sacraments.

CHAPTER SEVEN

••• Mothers Celebrate

On the other side of the north wall of my kitchen, I have a unique domestic space that we call the mudroom. It serves not only as a second, more utilitarian entrance to the house, but also as a storage area for special-occasion items that have nowhere else to go. Kitchen appliances that I only use from time to time line the shelves, along with vases, oversized platters, and festive bowls. Disposable party-ware occupies a corner next to the pancake griddle just below the stack of coolers. Balloons, crepe paper, and birthday banners also reside in this sphere.

So, whenever we have a party, host a dinner, or plan a picnic, I pop in and out of the mudroom to access these special items. And as each holiday rolls around, I step into this glorified supply closet to access the clear plastic bins filled with all of our Christmas, Easter, Thanksgiving, Fourth of July, Halloween, Valentine's, and St. Patrick's Day decorations. When those go up, the "regular" decorations come down and take up their temporary residence here among the seasonal supplies.

Prior to my arrival, this hallwayesque room didn't have much of an identity. It certainly hadn't enjoyed any attention from my husband, who had lived in this old farmhouse for several years already. A rickety, orange wooden door to the outside hung crook-edly off its hinges, letting in not only cold air but also a fair bit of dust and dirt from the hay field next door. The matted blue carpet was barely visible under the cover of aluminum cans awaiting recycling and the stash of ancient junk from the farm. During our engagement, Joe decided to use it as a pen for Marybelle, a Holstein calf born eight weeks prematurely that he took under his wing—and into the house! But when we got married, Marybelle moved out and I moved in. And I had a different vision for how this space would be used.

At my request, Joe remodeled the area for me, painting the walls, adding a system of shelves and hooks, and installing modern linoleum and a new door to the outside. The transformation was impressive, and very helpful. This refurbished space enabled us to store all of the party supplies that, believe it or not, showed up when I showed up. (Joe didn't have a party center, because Joe didn't have parties.)

We don't host gatherings all the time. But I do hold the belief that it's nice to be equipped to have a celebration when the opportunity arises. And while Joe is very happy to join me in such endeavors, I'm really the driving force behind the formal festivity in our family. I get out the streamers and make the signs. I hang the balloons in the morning before anyone wakes up. It's important to me to buy a present or two and have it wrapped and ready. I also like to host the party, which means planning the menu, shopping for the supplies, and cleaning the house.

My children love to help me with these tasks, whether it's for their own birthday or for one of their siblings. They look forward to it and count down the days on the calendar. That sense of excitement, joy, and expectation means a lot to me as their mother. I love it when my children experience life as a cause for celebration. I especially appreciate when they pour their energy and effort into planning someone else's party. To me, it feels like training them to be focused on bringing joy to others.

We celebrate more than birthdays, of course. As life unfolds, it presents many opportunities for rejoicing. My son's T-ball games give us a chance to cheer and congratulate him when he hits the ball instead of the tee. My oldest daughter's performance at the ballet recital earns her a bouquet of flowers and a round of hugs, while my youngest daughter's first finger painting leads us to do a happy dance in the dining room (after we wash our hands). When my second daughter has a successful session with her speech therapist, we celebrate with a little treat from the café. And when the baby first coos or smiles, I share the good news with the family and call them all over to marvel at his remarkable skills.

These moments truly make me proud. I have a deep desire to acknowledge the effort that went into these little accomplishments. My husband is equally devoted to our children, though I sometimes find myself nudging Joe in the arm a little, to encourage him to take his response up a notch. Joe knows when it's one of our children's birthdays. He gives them extra hugs and special greetings, and he uses the opportunity to tell them how glad he is that they were born. I know he's proud of the kids, too, but it seems that I'm usually the one who stirs up the celebrations in our family.

Based on my casual observations, I think I'm not alone in this regard. The countless family get-togethers I've attended over the years (with the exception of Mother's Day) were almost always spearheaded by the women. Moms are so often the first ones to clap and shout with glee as their children travel through the milestones of life. And we are frequently the driving force behind the more "major" celebrations of life as well.

Every holiday brings with it the chance to relish the rhythms and rituals of human existence, whether we're measuring the movement of the year with certain decorations, or doing a bit of special cooking with the kids (pink cupcakes for Valentine's Day or green oatmeal for breakfast on St. Patrick's Day).

At our house, the children love it when we celebrate the feast days of our favorite saints. We pull our saint picture books off the shelf, take a close look at any medals, statues, or holy cards we have to remind us of our patrons, and do a fun craft or cooking project. One year on the feast day of St. George, I made a green dragon-shaped cake and let the kids slay it with butter knives. We talked about how the dragon is like sin and the knife is like virtue. Such activities offer a chance both to teach the children and to have some good old-fashioned fun. It creates memories and establishes bonds of joy in the family. That alone makes it all worth the effort.

Of course Christmas provides the most extensive and elaborate opportunity for decoration, preparation, and education. The lights and ornaments on the tree, the special figurines in the nativity set, the musical snowmen, and the collection of seasonal candles and books all help to make our home a special yuletide wonderland. No other feeling is quite like the glee of taking out these familiar treasures every year and finding just the right place to set them up. Listening to Christmas carols in the background, breaking out the eggnog for the first time, and frosting Christmas cookies add to the magic. All of this provides countless opportunities to talk to the children about family traditions and teach them about the real meaning of Christmas.

I have a few guidelines that go along with all these celebrations. No Christmas decorations before Advent, because the season is meant to be about the coming of Jesus. No Halloween celebration without attention to All Saints' Day, which is where this favorite fall holiday has its origin. No Fourth of July fireworks without singing "America the Beautiful," and so on.

These traditions help each event to maintain its substance and meaning. Celebration without justification can become empty. It can be emptied of its fullest potential when it is separated from the underlying cause for joy. This is why it's also important to me to have periods of time when there aren't any special decorations around or any parties on the calendar. Without these pauses between celebrations, the festivity wouldn't be nearly as festive. In ecclesiastical language, we call these breaks "Ordinary Time." Although some people may not realize it and others may ignore it, many of our holiday celebrations are connected to the life of the Church.

Mother Church Celebrates

Originally, a holiday was a *holy* day. The Church established these holy days—often called feast days—and the people celebrated accordingly. In our day and age, religious value is often separated from holidays even when their origins are ecclesiastical; Christmas and Easter are cases in point. But it's important to remember that Mother Church wants her children to celebrate! She has established an entire cycle of celebrations, in fact, which we call the liturgical year.

The United States Conference of Catholic Bishops explains the annual cycle in this way:

> The liturgical year is made up of six seasons:
> Advent—four weeks of preparation before the celebration of Jesus' birth.
>
> Christmas Time—recalling the Nativity of Jesus Christ and his manifestation to the peoples of the world.
>
> Lent—a six-week period of penance before Easter.
>
> Sacred Paschal Triduum—the holiest "Three Days" of the Church's year, where the Christian people recall the suffering, death, and resurrection of Jesus.
>
> Easter Time—fifty days of joyful celebration of the Lord's resurrection from the dead and his sending forth of the Holy Spirit.
>
> Ordinary Time—divided into two sections (one span of 4–8 weeks after Christmas Time and another lasting about six months after Easter Time), wherein the faithful consider the fullness of Jesus' teachings and works among his people.[59]

Each of these seasons has its own special character. And the Church, in her maternal manner, sees to it that every church building is decorated accordingly. So it is that the vestments of the priest and the linens in the sanctuary all correspond to a certain color scheme according to the liturgical season.

In Advent, the color is purple (listed as "violet" on the official calendar put out by the USCCB). Typically, the church hangs or displays a large Advent wreath, complete with one candle for each Sunday of Advent—usually three purple and one pink. Many people choose to join in this tradition by having their own Advent wreath at home. For my family, this wreath sits on our dining room table during those weeks before Christmas. It helps to remind us every day that we are preparing ourselves for the coming of Christ.

White, often with gold, is worn and displayed when the great feast of Christmas finally arrives. Many churches throughout the world also mark this season with a splendid array of decorations. Christmas trees, bright red and white poinsettias, gold-ribboned wreaths, and, of course, the manger scene that hosts the Holy Family usually make their appearance to augment the celebration.

The time and effort we spend preparing our own homes for Christmas is a kind of participation in this larger effort put forth by the universal Church. Traditionally, the family has been called "the domestic church."[60] Our sharing in these rituals of celebration within our homes is one way that this title seems very fitting.

After the end of the Christmas season, when Ordinary Time returns, the priest puts on his green vestment as the nativity set is packed away, the wreaths are taken down, and the remaining poinsettias are distributed to parishioners. So too, in our homes, we box up the yuletide supplies and return to our default decorating scheme. Then, just when Ordinary Time is beginning to wear on us for being a bit too long, Ash Wednesday makes its appearance, ushering in the beginning of Lent.

Purple is again the color of choice for the Lenten season of penitence and preparation. According to the USCCB calendar, the forty days of violet are only interrupted three times: white for the feast of St. Joseph on March 19, and again for the Annunciation later in March, and "rose" on the fourth Sunday of Lent (Laetare Sunday), when the liturgical mood allows for a bit of mid-Lent rejoicing ("We're halfway there!").

Laetare Sunday, by the way, enjoys an interesting history as "Mothering Sunday." In a tradition dating back to the sixteenth century, the faithful would visit their "mother church"—usually the local cathedral—on this day in Lent.[61] Those who made the pilgrimage were said to have gone "a-mothering." The practice expanded in later years to allow for young servants to take a day off to return to their mother church back home.

> In the Middle Ages in England, boys and girls who lived away from home (as apprentices, servants, etc.) were allowed on mid-Lent Sunday, as it was called, to go home to visit their "mother church," where they had been baptized or had been brought up (the church which had given them spiritual birth in baptism was known as the "mother church"). They brought gifts to be placed on the altar and then visited their own mothers, bringing them flowers and cakes and doing all the housework for them![62]

How appropriate that it was loyalty to the importance of the "mother church" that led to this celebration of motherhood! Mothering Sunday is still observed in England, though now it is more of a parallel to the American Mother's Day. Although few people are aware of it, the idea of the annual tribute to mothers was first established through the Church.

Following Laetare Sunday, the violet continues until Holy Week, which begins with the dramatic red of Palm Sunday. On this day anyone who walks into a Catholic church will be handed a fresh green palm to carry with them as they process with the entire congregation in memory of Jesus's triumphal entry into Jerusalem. This special celebration, often called "Passion Sunday," is meant to give us the feeling of being among the throngs of people who waved palm branches and cried, "Hosanna!" as Jesus came near them. Many Catholics keep the blessed palms in their homes for the entire year until the next Ash Wednesday, when the palms are burned and used for anointing with ashes.

On the heels of Holy Week comes Easter. Now white is the color of choice, with the occasional appearance of red, all the way through to Pentecost, which concludes the Easter season with one last burst of red before the return to "ordinary" green. Pentecost commemorates the coming of the Holy Spirit upon the apostles after Jesus had risen from the dead and ascended into heaven. In remembrance of the tongues of fire that came down from the Holy Spirit, we use red for this holy day.

I recall our parish celebration of Pentecost from my grade school days, when everyone was invited to the gym after Mass to drink red punch and eat cake with red-frosting letters, and to launch red balloons and join together in praying for an outpouring of the Holy Spirit. The punch and balloons might seem superfluous, but they sure helped me remember Pentecost!

Our celebrations really can be educational and formative. What we choose to "party" about reveals what's important to us. So often, we celebrate to commemorate. We recall anniversaries, birthdays, and sometimes other significant occasions in our families' lives in order to give these moments their due respect. The Church does the same throughout the liturgical year as she celebrates not just the "big" holidays but a host of other important events.

August, for example, commemorates the Transfiguration of the Lord (6), the Assumption of the Blessed Virgin Mary (15), the Queenship of the Blessed Virgin Mary (22), and the Passion of

St. John the Baptist (29). This is in addition to the feast days of great saints that fall in the same month, such as Alphonsus Ligouri, Dominic, Clare, John Vianney, Maximilian Kolbe, Edith Stein, and Monica and her son, Augustine. What a lineup!

We can also experience our own parish churches as centers of local community celebrations. Of course, the most fundamental "family" gathering of our faith is the Eucharistic meal. Similar to so many mothers who gather their husband and children together for family dinners, Mother Church gathers her children together every Sunday to celebrate this holy feast.

Around the table of the altar, we join with our fellow Catholics, our neighbors, and our friends to be fed by the Lord. We celebrate together, not alone. In this way, Mother Church keeps our faith from being a solitary experience. If there were no Church, there would be no real *community* of believers. We might have our personal "spirituality," but we would lack the support, the fellowship, and the mutual encouragement that comes from belonging to a family of faith.

The parish family also celebrates other occasions, such as baptisms and First Communions, as everyone joins together to welcome new members into the fold. Weddings are in many cases still a parish-based celebration as well. Then there are the church picnics, the donuts and coffee after Mass, the summer festivals, the fundraising dinners and date nights, and sometimes even cultural celebrations with guest musicians or artists who share their talents at a local church. Although not happy occasions, funeral dinners also offer an opportunity for the community to gather and support the grieving families in their midst.

Depending on the particular parish atmosphere, the church often becomes a vital social gathering place. Even the chatting and visiting that takes place outside of the front doors after Mass is a way that the Church allows us to celebrate as we share our stories and catch up with one another. For those parishioners who are authentically invested in their community, their church building itself becomes a kind of home.

In many cases, it is the mother who tends to the atmosphere of the home. Rare is the mother who doesn't have a fair bit of influence over the way her house is decorated. Each woman has her own taste and style that contributes to the "feel" of the house, helping to create the environment that her children will associate with the very idea of "home."

When I was growing up, my mother had certain pictures around the house, like Jean-Honoré Fragonard's *A Young Girl Reading*. Without fail, a sense of comfort and familiarity always washes over me when I see that image of the elegant woman in her yellow dress, gazing contentedly at the little red book in her hands. And it's not because of the painting itself. It's because that painting is like a window into the joys of my childhood home.

So too, the way that a church is decorated, the design of the space, the images on the stained-glass windows, the statues in the alcoves, the warmth of the gathering spaces, even the smell in the air—all of these things contribute to the feeling of "home" that our churches convey. The diversity is vast in this regard, from the magnificent, echoing grandeur of the mosaic-laden Basilica of the Immaculate Conception in Washington, DC, to the humble simplicity of the small rural parishes that dot the Midwestern countryside.

Whatever the degree of the decor, the sights and smells and sounds of our churches—if, in fact, we spend enough time in them— become familiar and comfortable to us. The physical building, the aesthetics, and the atmosphere, as so many moms know, really do make a difference. In its own variety of homecoming, when we step inside the doors of "our" church, we can tangibly feel the welcoming embrace of Mother Church.

Another Mother's Voice: Yvonne's Story

Yvonne is the mother of one daughter and two sons, and the grandmother of eight. She is the mother of a priest.

When I think of my mother, I think of being home. Home—a place of unconditional welcome! For me, in spite of times of confusion, questions, and concerns, the Catholic Church is home. Mother Church has many of the same qualities as my childhood home; both are places of welcome and love, traditions and memories, and loving relationships.

I think another part of why the Church is home is because, in many church buildings, time and money and love have been invested to make them places of beauty to honor our Lord, and places of rest, peace, and welcome. Beautiful buildings, art, and music are part of our heritage.

In the Old Testament, God laid out detailed directions for the beauty and holiness of his home. Church buildings, by their beauty, remind me of the awesome splendor of our God! I like to think that, even in our modern world of hurry and rush, there is a place—an actual building—where beauty and splendor and holiness are important. We American homemakers spend much money and many hours decorating our homes so they will be welcoming and warm and wonderful for all who enter. Mother Church does this for us, too.

Along the way, the Church has helped me "build" my own home. One way she did this was through the gift of God's Word that she has given us. As a young mother of three small children, I was overwhelmed by choices, confused about decisions, and just plain tired! So I became involved in a number of Bible studies that were support groups for moms.

My very first Bible study was called "The Philosophy of Christian Womanhood." A theme of this study was the crucial role a wife can play in the success or failure of a happy and godly home. At the time the ideas were new to me, and now I suspect many women would think them foolish and antiquated. But from my viewpoint of forty-five years of happy marriage, I would suggest that God's Word leads us to truth if we are willing to listen and try to obey.

I took our third child along with me to that study when he was a newborn. Now, he is a priest with a doctorate in Scripture studies! So I can say that his first exposure to the Bible happened while he was literally sitting in his baby seat.

My husband and I are so truly blessed to be parents of a son of the Church. I do not think I can put into simple words the feelings that overwhelmed me on the day of his ordination. Watching our son prostrate himself before God on the altar, and then being lovingly and personally blessed and thanked by our son immediately after his ordination Mass, brought such tears of joy and gratitude.

I did not realize it until that day, but Mother Church has a beautiful tradition that honors the mothers of her priests. It involves a small piece of white linen, called the Maniturgium. This is the cloth that the ordaining bishop uses to consecrate the new priest's hands with sacred oil. The white linen represents the burial shroud of Christ that protected his body in the tomb. Traditionally this cloth is given to the mother of the priest because she was the first protector of this newly ordained priest in her womb.

My son gave his Maniturgium to me, embroidered with his name on it, after his ordination. He told me that the mother of a priest is buried with this cloth. Until then, it is framed and hanging up in our home. But when I die, it will be placed around my hands to affirm that I have given my son to serve Jesus and our Church as a priest.

I remember making this "gift" of my son very concretely. In the first year after his ordination, I was able to dedicate him to Mary and to the service of *her* Son while kneeling next to my son at Mary's home in Nazareth. When he received an assignment in Jerusalem after his ordination, we were able to visit our son in the Holy Land. We stopped to pray at the small home of Mary, the simple home where the angel Gabriel appeared to her. There, where Gabriel spoke the words, "Do not be afraid," I made my dedication. I asked that Mary watch over my son as she watched over her own Son, Jesus. I truly felt that Mary would take him under her care and protection.

How fitting that it was in the context of a "home" that I entrusted my son to Mary, the Mother of the Church.

• What elements of Yvonne's story resonate with your own? What touched, surprised, or inspired you about her reflection?

• Take a few moments to ponder or journal about how you have experienced the Church's motherly "celebration" in your life. Then, turn to the study guide on page 122 for further reflection from the lives of the saints, the teaching of the Church, the liturgy, and the sacraments.

CHAPTER EIGHT ··· Mary, for Mothers

Just before I sat down to write this section, I was nursing my baby boy. As I cradled him, gazing down while he peacefully faded off to sleep, I found myself thinking about God's wisdom. What a beautiful way to create human beings—as babies! What a brilliant design that makes every single person's beginning into an experience of such humble dependence. We need one another. Truly, we cannot live without other people.

Although we often forget this as self-sufficient adults, it only takes a moment of encounter with a baby to remind us. The obvious incapacity to function alone and the innocent trust of these tiny humans should bring us all back to our roots. We all began this way and owe our existence to interdependence, particularly with our mothers.

As I meditated upon these thoughts, it struck me that when the Son of God became man it was not *necessary* that he show up as an infant. I suppose I had always imagined that if God was going to be a human, he had no choice but to begin as a baby. That's how humans start, after all. But this afternoon I thought of it from a different angle.

God could have done things differently. He has the power to appear in any way he wants to at any time he so chooses. However, in his eternal wisdom, he decided that the fulcrum of human history was best situated in the context of a woman and her child. God *chose* to come by means of motherhood. And so, he was conceived in a woman's womb.

I began to reflect upon the infant Jesus, cradled in his Mother's lap as a little baby boy—so much like the one who was now drawing nourishment and comfort from my body. Think of it—how amazing it is that Mary nourished and comforted her Savior. How remarkable that our Creator should be so humble. *God* chose to *submit* to a *woman*. God decided to have a mother.

Our reflections on motherhood and the Church wouldn't be complete without turning to the woman whom God chose for this incredible task. So we will conclude our reflections by considering some concrete ways that the Blessed Mother can assist us in our vocation. To this end, we will look at seven different titles of Mary and explore what these titles reveal to us.

Mother of God

Most of us are so used to hearing Mary referred to as the Mother of God that we hardly bat an eyelash at the title. But this wasn't always so. Great debates took place in the early Church to establish this noble name.

In the year 431, at the Council of Ephesus, the Church formally declared that Mary was the *Theotokos*, Greek for "God-bearer" and popularly rendered as "Mother of God." This was in contrast to the position of Nestorius, then Bishop of Constantinople. He believed Mary was the mother of Christ only in Christ's humanity, not in his divinity. Thus, Nestorius wanted to do away with the already longstanding title of Mary as *Theotokos*.

But Mother Church knew better. To deny that Mary was the Mother of God was to suggest that there were two Christs. But Jesus Christ is one person, fully human and fully divine.

Had the Nestorian heresy taken root, there would have been another consequence. It would have detracted from the dignity of motherhood. Because the Church insisted that Mary was the Mother of God, the Church also implicitly affirmed the exalted role of motherhood in the work of salvation. A woman was given the extraordinary task of conceiving God in her womb and bearing him to the world.

This astonishing Christian doctrine should inject us with confidence! Our motherhood is wrapped in tremendous dignity. Any argument to the contrary has no place in the Christian worldview. As mothers we have a share in the vocation of Mary, although her mission was certainly unique—she is, after all, both the Blessed Mother and the Blessed Virgin!

Pope St. John Paul II reflects on this marvelous reality in *Mulieris Dignitatem*. There he comments on "virginity and motherhood as two particular dimensions of the fulfillment of the female personality," and he notes:

> These *two dimensions of the female vocation* were united in [Mary] in an exceptional manner.... Indeed, the person of the Mother of God helps everyone—especially women—to see how these two dimensions, these two paths in the vocation of women as persons, explain and complete each other.[63]

The fact remains that, through Mary, God has greatly exalted motherhood. Mary brought the only Son of the Father into the world and nurtured him physically and emotionally. We also play an irreplaceable role as we bring children of God into the world and nurture them through our maternal gifts.

When society wants to downplay the importance of our work as mothers, when culture suggests that we ought to be doing something different with our lives, or when the daily grind of motherhood doesn't appear to mean anything worthwhile, let's stop and remember that God chose to have a mom.

Daughter of Thy Son

Dante, the great Italian author of the famous *Divine Comedy*, poetically referred to Mary as "Daughter of Thy Son."[64] At first a puzzling phrase, it is nonetheless beautiful and profound on a deeper level. Of course Mary was Christ's Mother, but because Christ is God, Mary is also his daughter, a child of God as we all are. Indeed, Mary was a child of God *par excellence*. She was the first and the best disciple of the Son of God, even though he was her Son. Perhaps we could actually say *because* he was her Son.

Mary knew Jesus better than anyone else. Like other mothers, she was the first to encounter and know her child through the intimacy of conception and gestation in her womb. She accompanied Jesus through every moment of his infancy and childhood, and she ushered him into adulthood. She—more than his closest friends, more than his twelve chosen apostles—understood his thoughts, his expressions, his gestures, and his tendencies. If anyone had a clear view into the mind of Christ, it was his Mother, Mary.

So her ability to follow him, to learn from him, to orient her life around his teachings and his truth, was augmented by her blessed maternity. It was in part this very motherhood that made Mary such an excellent "daughter" of God.

Mary had the humility—and the wisdom—to allow herself to learn from her child. And as mothers, we are called to do the same. The children God entrusts to our care are not just there for us to guide, nurture, and form. God gives us these particular people, these sons and daughters, to enrich us. I believe he brings these unique, unrepeatable souls with these special gifts, talents, and sensitivities into our lives in part because he knows we need them!

God knows that my son's irrepressible cheerfulness and long-suffering patience are qualities that I ought to imitate. He knows that my daughter's physical affection and creative energy are gifts that balance out my tendency toward dry efficiency and impersonal productivity. Each of my children bring special characteristics to our home that help us all to be more well-rounded, better people. And my oldest is just eight! I can only imagine the amount of learning and growth that is still in store for me as my children grow and mature.

Like Mary, we are invited to mature alongside our children, to accept each son and daughter as free individuals, and to welcome their unique mission. We are called to have the humility to allow our children to teach us as we journey through life together. In this way, each mother can become the "daughter" of her sons—and daughters.

The New Eve

The first woman was called Eve "because she was the mother of all living" (Genesis 3:20). But, alas, Eve's deadly choice in the Garden of Eden scarred her life-giving mission. Instead of following God's design, she fell for the design of the devilish serpent. Thus, sin entered the picture, and all of the children of Eve, ever since, have been born into a fallen world.

But Mary, through her life-giving yes to God, bore the Savior who crushes the head of the serpent (cf. Genesis 3:15) and redeems this fallen world. As the Second Vatican Council explained, "through her faith and obedience she gave birth on earth to the very Son of the Father...in the manner of a New Eve who placed her faith, not in the serpent of old but in God's messenger."[65]

In the second century, St. Irenaeus had already reflected on this theme. "The knot of Eve's disobedience was untied by Mary's obedience," he wrote. "What the virgin Eve bound through her disbelief, Mary loosened by her faith" (CCC, 494). A few centuries later, St. Jerome, the great Bible scholar and doctor of the Church, put it simply: "Death through Eve, life through Mary" (CCC, 494).

The profound Catholic recognition of Mary's significance and her irreplaceable role in salvation history is a powerful counterpoint to the unfortunate image of Eve. Anyone who mistakenly believes that Catholics think women are inferior creatures only has to look to the theology of Mary to realize that this isn't so. As Pope St. John Paul II said, "The figure of Mary shows that God has such esteem for woman that any form of discrimination lacks a theoretical basis."[66]

The Eve-Mary contrast presents motherhood from two different perspectives. Eve made her decisions based on what would serve *her*: "So when the woman saw that the tree was good for food, and that it was a delight to the eyes, and that the tree was to be desired to make one wise, she took of its fruit and ate" (Genesis 3:6). Mary, on the other hand, made her decisions based on what would serve *God*, humbly identifying herself as the handmaid of the Lord and praying her beautiful hymn from Luke's Gospel, the Magnificat. Pope Emeritus Benedict XVI put it well in his encyclical letter *Deus Caritas Est* (God is Love), "Mary's greatness consists in the fact that she wants to magnify God, not herself."[67]

Navigating the responsibilities of motherhood is no simple task. We want to do what's right, but we are also tempted to do what's easy. Sometimes we might wish there was a simple formula to guide our choices, but in fact we cannot reduce motherhood to a rigid code of behavior or a stereotypical set of motherly duties. Even the seven themes of this book cannot possibly encompass all that mothers do for their children or enumerate the vast diversity of gifts that individual mothers possess. Every mother has been given her own set of talents and her own unique mission within her maternal vocation.

As we try to discern how best to live out this vocation in our particular situation, it might be helpful to look to these two mothers. When a decision is in front of us, we can ask ourselves: "What would Eve do here, and what would Mary do?" Imagining Mary in our concrete circumstances can free us from acting based on social expectations or predetermined formulas. Steering clear of the selfishness and pride of Eve will also serve us well. Choosing instead to be Marian mothers will help us follow God's unique plan for our lives, moment by moment and day by day.

Our Mother of Perpetual Help

One Saturday afternoon, at the end of a talk I gave to a group of moms on the subject of Mary and motherhood, a young mother in the front row made a challenging comment. "It's all very lovely to reflect on Mary like this, but after a while I just find it tiresome," she confessed honestly. "I'm so far from being like Mary that it just makes me feel worse to talk about how amazing she was."

The nods from around the room confirmed that many other moms agreed with her. As mothers, we are often so aware of our failings and weaknesses! Besides the duties and demands we can never seem to master, many of us compare ourselves to other moms and feel inferior. We judge ourselves harshly and feel guilty. We regret the wrong choices that we can't undo. We wish things were perfect for our children, but we know they're not.

Most of us have a "laundry" list of what a good mother is supposed to be, and we often feel that we don't deserve the title. We compare ourselves to our mothers for better or for worse. We try to live up to standards from society, the Church, our husbands, families, peers, coworkers, and even our children, who are often the first to criticize our mothering either in their words or through their actions.

This young woman's comment resonated with me as much as anyone. Yes, if we only think of Mary as yet another impossible standard, then it's tempting to avoid her altogether. But Mary is not just a model for us. She is a *mother* for us. As Pope Benedict XVI wrote:

> The words addressed by the crucified Lord to his disciple—to John and through him to all disciples of Jesus: "Behold, your mother!" (John 19:27)—are fulfilled anew in every generation. Mary has truly become the Mother of all believers. Men and women of every time and place have recourse to her motherly kindness and her virginal purity and grace, in

all their needs and aspirations, their joys and sorrows, their moments of loneliness and their common endeavors.[68]

Mary is our companion. She is our intercessor. She is here to *help* us, not to judge us. It would be foolish to avoid her simply because she is such a good mother! As St. Anthony of Padua preached, Mary offers "solace to the afflicted and hope to the despairing."[69] Thus we can turn to her precisely in our moments of *weakness* and ask her to help us find guidance and wisdom and support, just as so many of us do with our own mothers.

Because Mary already dwells in heaven, we can turn to her at any time and ask her to pray for us. This is what we do when we call upon Mary as Our Mother of Perpetual Help. *Perpetual* means unending, untiring, ongoing, there when we need it. That's the kind of assistance Mary offers us, her children.

This particular devotion has its origin in connection with a sacred icon of Mary holding the infant Jesus. The original image hangs in the Church of St. Alphonsus Ligouri in Rome, but blessed replicas of the icon are now widespread throughout the world thanks to the work of the religious order he founded, the Redemptorists. In fact, during the year that I am writing this book—the 150th jubilee of the icon being entrusted to the Redemptorists—Pope Francis has granted a plenary indulgence[70] in conjunction with making a pilgrimage to any Redemptorist church to visit the icon of Our Mother of Perpetual Help. Why would we want or need to receive an indulgence? Pope Francis explains indulgences in his apostolic letter *Misericordiae Vultus*:

> In the Sacrament of Reconciliation, God forgives our sins, which he truly blots out; and yet sin leaves a negative effect on the way we think and act. But the mercy of God is stronger even than this. It becomes indulgence on the part of the Father who, through the Bride of Christ, his Church, reaches the pardoned sinner and frees him from every residue left by

the consequences of sin, enabling him to act with charity, to grow in love rather than to fall back into sin.... To gain an indulgence is to experience the holiness of the Church, who bestows upon all the fruits of Christ's redemption, so that God's love and forgiveness may extend everywhere.[71]

We need not be in front of the sacred image to seek Mary's prayers, of course. We can turn to her right in the midst of our mothering with words like these, or whatever else may spring to our lips:

Mother of Perpetual Help, you have been blessed and favored by God. You became not only the Mother of the Redeemer, but Mother of the redeemed as well. We come to you today as your loving children. Watch over us and take care of us. As you held the child Jesus in your loving arms, so take us in your arms. Be a mother ready at every moment to help us. For God who is mighty has done great things for you, and God's mercy is from age to age on those who love God. Intercede for us, dear Mother, in obtaining pardon for our sins, love for Jesus, final perseverance, and the grace always to call upon you. Mother of Perpetual Help, pray for me and grant me the favor I confidently ask of you {mention your petition}.[72]

Undoer of Knots

Empathy is a gift. Through it, we enter into the experience of the people that we love. When they rejoice, we rejoice. But when they suffer, we suffer. Like Mary whose heart was "pierced" when her Son was pierced, as mothers we tend to take on the pain of our families and our children in particular. Unfortunately, sometimes this pain can be tremendous.

Most of us can relate to the idea of having a "knot in our stomach" when it comes to difficult situations in which there seems to be no way out, or in which we desperately want to help but don't know what to do. As we saw in our reflection on Mary as the New Eve, St. Irenaeus referred to "the knot" of sin that Mary untied through her faith. So we turn to Mary as the Undoer of Knots and ask for her prayers to untangle the knots in our lives and in the lives of those we care about. What are some examples of these knots? In *Understanding Mary, Undoer of Knots*, we read:

> The thorny problems that Mary can "untie" include situations we encounter that seem to have no solutions—marital or family difficulties caused by violence, drug or alcohol abuse, lack of employment, depression, abortion, illness, addictions to social media or pornography, the grief and distress experienced by separated couples or rupture of the family, or any occurrence that would disrupt the peace of home life.[73]

The devotion to Mary, Undoer of Knots, has gained quick popularity since Pope Francis brought it to the world's attention in conjunction with his admiration for a German painting by this title. The painting by Johann Schmidtner was commissioned after the successful resolution of a domestic difficulty that took place early in the eighteenth century. A certain Austrian couple on the verge of divorce went for counsel to a Jesuit priest who held the couple's white wedding ribbon up to an image of Mary and prayed for help. Thanks to Mary's intercession, the couple experienced peace, and their marriage was saved.

In thanksgiving for this answered prayer, the couple's grandson donated the beautiful painting of "Mary, Undoer of Knots" to the Church of St. Peter am Perlach in Augsburg, Bavaria. The work of art depicts Mary untying a knot from a long white wedding ribbon. The piece of ribbon that she has not yet touched hangs gnarled and tangled at her side, but the half that has passed through her hands is a perfectly smooth flowing garland. The image gives a striking visual representation of the power of Mary's intercession.

Isn't this exactly what we want to happen to the knots we can't untangle? We want someone to help turn the rat's nest into a ribbon. Next time we find ourselves at a complete loss for what to do to help our loved ones, may we remember to entrust the situation to the holy hands of Mary, Undoer of Knots.

Star of the Sea

One of the earliest references to Mary as *Stella Maris,* Star of the Sea, dates back to the year 865: "Mary, Star of the Sea, must be followed in faith and morals lest we capsize amidst the storm-tossed waves of the sea. She will illumine us to believe in Christ, born of her for the salvation of the world."[74]

Like the bright North Star that once directed sailors adrift at sea, the devotion to Mary, Star of the Sea, understands Our Lady as a guiding star leading us always toward Jesus. Her mission is forever his mission. Her goal is to lead her children to her Son. Think of the wedding feast at Cana where Mary gave the simple instruction, "Do whatever he tells you" (John 2:5). Mary helps us keep our focus on Jesus.

This, of course, is the most important thing we can do as mothers. When we orient our lives around Jesus, who is "the way, and the truth, and the life" (John 14:6), we will not get lost. When we keep him at the center of our hearts and our homes, we will become the best mothers we can be. But if we lose sight of him, allowing the demands of daily life to distract us, then our family will suffer as a result.

We can come up with any number of lists of what it means to be a mother. We can talk about the seven themes of this book—creating and caring and teaching and healing and the rest—but without the love of Christ at the center of it all, these actions become what St. Paul called "a noisy gong or a clanging cymbal" (1 Corinthians 13:1). Motherhood without the love of Christ loses its full beauty.

But Mary helps us to create beautiful maternal music because she shows us how to be mothers who love the Lord.

Mary has walked the very path we are on. She knows what it is to be a mother, to make a home, to raise a child, to share life with a husband. She has done all of this before us, and now from her vantage point in heaven she looks upon us with tender compassion and concern. We in turn can look to her, as a bright star in the spiritual sky, for guidance and direction. Especially when we are plagued by doubt or despair in matters of faith, we can ask Mary to help steer us on the right course.

As St. Bernard of Clairvaux instructs us, "If the winds of temptation arise; If you are driven upon the rocks of tribulation look to the star, call on Mary; If you are tossed upon the waves of pride, of ambition, of envy, of rivalry, look to the star, call on Mary."[75]

Mother of the Church

Even Mother Church has a mother! Pope St. John Paul II developed the theology behind the Marian title "Mother of the Church" following in the footsteps of several of his predecessors. In a catechesis on the Blessed Virgin, he said:

> The title "Mother of the Church" reflects the deep conviction of the Christian faithful, who see in Mary not only the mother of the person of Christ, but also of the faithful. She who is recognized as mother of salvation, life and grace, mother of the saved and mother of the living, is rightly proclaimed Mother of the Church.[76]

In other words, Mary is a spiritual mother to all believers who together make up the Church. So mothers are not the only ones called to follow Mary's example and enjoy her assistance! All Christians, all members of the body of Christ, can turn to her as their mother. So it is that the Church herself looks to Mary to enlighten her own self-understanding. As Pope Francis said in a catechesis about Mother Church, "The Church and the Virgin Mary are mothers, both of them; what is said of the Church can be said also of Our Lady and what is said of Our Lady can also be said of the Church!"[77]

On this theme, the Dogmatic Constitution on the Church, *Lumen Gentium* (The Light of the Nations), has a section dedicated to "The Blessed Virgin Mary, Mother of God in the Mystery of Christ and the Church." The document states:

> But while in the most Blessed Virgin the Church has already reached that perfection whereby she exists without spot or wrinkle (cf. Eph. 5:27), the faithful still strive to conquer sin and increase in holiness. And so they turn their eyes to Mary who shines forth to the whole community of the elect as the model of virtues.... In her life the Virgin has been a model of *that motherly love with which all* who join in the Church's apostolic mission for the regeneration of mankind *should be animated.*[78]

Everyone who participates in the mission of the Church should be moved by maternal love! Mary helps us understand maternal love at its best. As we have seen, her receptivity to God's action was the beginning of her holy maternity.

Pope Benedict XVI describes how she cooperated with God: "Mary is the mother and model of the Church who receives the divine Word in faith and offers herself to God as the 'good soil' in which he can continue to accomplish his mystery of salvation."[79] All Christians are called to imitate Mary by being the "good soil" or fertile ground that "bears fruit and yields, in one case a hundredfold, in another sixty, and in another thirty" (Matthew 13:23). In our case, this fertility is made manifest in and through our motherhood!

Our children, the fruit of our womb, become the hundredfold reward of our efforts when we keep them rooted in Christ and his Church. This is *our* mission. But thank God, we're not in it alone. Along with all the benefits we receive from Mother Church, we have the Blessed Mother to help us along the way. After all, our children are Mary's children, too. As Pope Paul VI declared, "The Holy Mother of God, the new Eve, Mother of the Church, continues in heaven to exercise her maternal role on behalf of the members of Christ."[80]

Mary, Mother of the Church, pray for us!

Another Mother's Voice: Mother Teresa of Calcutta

Mother Teresa was the spiritual mother of thousands of children. (These reflections, which are taken from several of Mother Teresa's speeches found in the book *One Heart Full of Love,* help us understand the Marian devotion that was such an integral part of Mother Teresa's spiritual motherhood.)

Above all, we are deeply grateful to Mother Church for allowing us to live our vocation…. God still loves the world and today he continues to give Jesus to the world through you and me.

…God gave his Son to Mary, the virgin immaculate. The very moment she said that she was the handmaid of the Lord and confessed her lowliness, saying that she was nothing, she was filled with grace. We know what happened afterwards. She began carrying Jesus in her womb, and she wanted to share him right away with others. She went as the servant of the Lord, even serving as his slave. She went in haste, as if there were not enough time, to share Jesus with others. We, too, must do the same. For her the day of the annunciation was her First Communion Day. Jesus came into her life, and she wanted to immediately share him with others. So should it be with us.

Jesus has become the Bread of Life so that we too, just like Mary, may carry him. We too, just like Mary, must be ready to go in haste to share the Jesus we bear with others. Like her, we must try to serve others with the presence of Christ.

...I believe we must look for holiness, joy and love in our own homes. We must make our home like a second "Nazareth" where Jesus can come and live with us. Holiness is not a luxury, meant for only a few. It is a simple duty for each one of us. Holiness is to take whatever Jesus gives us and to give Jesus whatever he asks of us with a big smile. That is God's will.

...You and I must be carriers of God's love. Each time we receive Holy Communion we are filled with Jesus and we must, like our Lady, leave in haste and search out that run-away child and bring him home. We must bring him to where there is love, joy, peace— to the place where God is with us.

...We have a mother in heaven, the Virgin Mary, who is a guide for us, a great joy, and an important source of our cheerfulness in Christ. Intercede with her before God. Pray the rosary so that Mary may always be with you, to be your guide, to protect and keep you as a mother. [81]

- What elements of Mother Teresa's story resonate with your own? What touched, surprised, or inspired you about her reflection?

- Take a few moments to ponder or journal about how you have experienced Mary as a companion in your life. Then, turn to the study guide on page 125 for further reflection from the lives of the saints, the teaching of the Church, the liturgy, and the sacraments.

Study Guide

Chapter One • • • Mothers Create

LESSONS FROM THE SAINTS

The Church, as the bride of Christ, cooperates with the Lord in all that she does. Christ and his Church together form the *totus Christus*—the whole Christ. As St. Augustine wrote, "'The Word was made flesh, and dwelt in us.' To that flesh the Church is joined, and so there is made the whole Christ, Head and body."[82] So she is not a mother by her own power; the Church's fruitfulness is the product of her union with Jesus. She engenders new children only with God's help.

Each of us can appreciate this kind of unitive fruitfulness. A woman conceives a child in her womb because she is first united to her child's father. And man and woman both become parents only because God chooses to make that physical union fruitful.

• It often feels natural to behave as though our children are our own possessions. But in truth, we are caretakers entrusted by God with these precious lives. How might parents have a disordered sense of ownership over their child(ren)?

• As a mother, have you pondered what it means that your child(ren) belong(s) to God? How can you grow in appreciating this reality?

LESSONS FROM THE CATECHISM

"The sheer gratuitousness of the grace of salvation is particularly manifest in infant Baptism" (CCC, 1250). In other words, infants clearly can't *earn* their salvation, but they receive this blessing nonetheless when they are baptized. The Church bestows this gift of grace freely.

• How do you most often respond when you give of your time, your attention, and your energy to your children? Do you give these things freely ("gratuitously"), or do you expect your child(ren) to earn these gifts through proper behavior, good performance, or expressions of gratitude?

• Have you ever found it difficult to accept the idea that the Church embraces and accepts you the way you are right now, just as a good mother does? Is it possible to resolve such feelings—and if so, how?

LESSONS FROM THE LITURGY

During the celebration of marriage, the Church prays these words: "By your providence and grace, O Lord, you accomplish the wonder of this twofold design: that, while the birth of children brings beauty to the world, their rebirth in Baptism gives increase to the Church."[83] As mothers, we participate in this amazing process. Bearing children makes the world a more beautiful place, and when we have our children baptized, we help the Church to flourish.

• Our mission as mothers goes beyond simply raising happy and healthy children. We are called to raise holy children, too, who know of their dignity as children of God. How often do you think about raising your child(ren) to be holy?

• What can you do to help your son(s) or daughter(s) embrace their identity as children of God?

THE SEVEN SACRAMENTS: BAPTISM

The spiritual reality of new birth for our souls, at the hands of Mother Church, feels refreshing like water, smells sweet like chrism, and shines brightly like the flame of the baptismal candle. In the embrace of Mother Church, the neophyte hears words of welcome and feels the touch of another human hand. These gestures and physical elements are some of the gifts that we receive from the Church. Instead of floating, unsecured in an abyss of abstract religious ideas, our faith gives us the comforting touch of a mother. (See pages 10–12.)

• Call to mind the baptism of your child(ren)—or your own

baptism, if you remember it. What were the most memorable moments?

• Which prayers or rites of the celebration made the biggest impression on you? Why?

THE SEVEN DEADLY SINS: PRIDE

• Having the power to co-create life is a remarkable gift. However, this power could make us prideful if we begin to think of ourselves as superior (or inferior) to others because of it, either because of our fruitfulness—or lack of it. How can we avoid this pitfall? The best way is through the intentional cultivation of that sin's "virtuous antidote"—in this case, humility.

• It is humility that allows us to trust God even with our fertility. How have you seen this humility lived out in your own life, or in the lives of other couples?

Chapter Two • • • Mothers Care

LESSONS FROM THE SAINTS

St. Teresa of Avila, a doctor of the Church, is well loved for her profound mystical writings and admired for her contribution to the reforms of the Carmelite Order. But for all of her spiritual accomplishments, she managed to maintain a very practical perspective. She believed that extraordinary accomplishments or remarkable gifts were not necessary to please Jesus. Rather, a heart full of love and a commitment to doing God's will are what matter.

She wrote, "The Lord does not look so much at the magnitude of anything we do as at the love with which we do it."[84] As mothers, our lives are full of the little things. The question is whether or not we are doing these tiny tasks with great love.

• Reflect on the duties of your daily routine. When you are going about the business of the day, do any chores or tasks tend to frustrate or upset you? If so, how could you transform these difficult duties into acts of love for Christ?

• If you work outside the home (or work from home), do you ever feel torn between the different facets of your vocation, in caring for your family's needs? How can you better express love and care in each area of responsibility?

LESSONS FROM THE CATECHISM

"Parents' respect and affection are expressed by the care and attention they devote to bringing up their young children and *providing for their physical and spiritual needs*" (CCC, 2228). Here the Church reminds us that even providing for basic bodily needs— brushing teeth, making meals, changing diapers, folding clothes— is part of showing respect and affection for our children. In addition to providing physical care for them, which changes as they get older, we are also called to attend to their spiritual care.

• Often, we think of showing affection only in terms of hugs, cuddles, or kisses. But in reality this concept is much broader. How would you explain what affection really is and does?

• Describe how taking care of a simple task for your child, or teaching a spiritual lesson to a son or daughter, could both be signs of affection.

LESSONS FROM THE LITURGY

On November 23, the feast day of the Mexican martyr Miguel Pro, the Church prays, "Our God and Father, who conferred upon your servant Blessed Miguel Agustín Pro the grace of ardently seeking your greater glory and the salvation of others, grant, through his intercession and example, that by faithfully and joyfully performing our daily duties and effectively assisting those around us, we may serve you with zeal and ever seek your glory."[85] We don't have to wait for November to roll around to pray for these things! Faithfully and joyfully performing our daily duties is meant to happen year-round.

• Reflect on how prayer can help you fulfill your obligations well, whether in the home or out in the world. Do you perform your daily duties joyfully? What tasks are the biggest struggle for you?

• If you work outside of the home, how can you ensure that your employment is also a way of serving God "with zeal" and "effectively assisting" your family?

THE SEVEN SACRAMENTS: ANOINTING OF THE SICK

This rite clearly encourages the warmth of human touch. This sacrament helps to satisfy our human need for real physical encounter with one another in moments of trial. A mother's care for her sick child inevitably involves touching him or her. Here again, through the ministry of her priests, Mother Church reaches out to touch her children. (See pages 17–24.)

• The sacrament of anointing of the sick involves prayers from a priest for spiritual healing as well as physical healing, if it be God's will. Have you ever received or witnessed the last rites of the Church? If so, describe your experience. If not, explain what you know about this sacrament.

• How is this sacrament maternal in nature?

THE SEVEN DEADLY SINS: SLOTH

• This vice is more commonly known as *laziness*. It is a kind of spiritual cancer that eats away at our finding any joy in our work. What are some ways we can battle the temptation to shirk our tasks and give in to laziness?

• What virtue do we need to practice to combat this toxic vice?

Chapter Three • • • Mothers Teach

LESSONS FROM THE SAINTS

In his encyclical letter *Mater et Magistra*, Pope St. John XXIII wrote, "Mother and Teacher of all nations—such is the Catholic Church in the mind of her Founder, Jesus Christ; to hold the world in an embrace of love, that men, in every age, should find in her their own completeness in a higher order of living, and their ultimate salvation."[86] So, to be mother and teacher is to hold people "in an embrace of love" that helps them find fulfillment.

• Reflect on how teaching your child(ren) is an expression of love. Then, think of the opposite for a moment. How would *not* teaching your child(ren) be a failure in love?

• What would they be deprived of without your guidance? How could it affect their future?

LESSONS FROM THE CATECHISM

"Through the grace of the sacrament of marriage, parents receive the responsibility and privilege of *evangelizing their children.* Parents should initiate their children at an early age into the mysteries of the faith of which they are the 'first heralds' for their children. They should associate them from their most tender years with the life of the Church. A wholesome family life can foster interior dispositions that are a genuine preparation for a living faith and remain a support for it throughout one's life" (CCC, 2225).

• Reflect upon your own early faith-formation experiences. How did you experience the maternal gift of teaching in your own life— through your own mother, or a spiritual mother?

• Reflect on being a "herald" of the faith for your child(ren). What do you think is most important to announce or proclaim about the faith? How can you best share these things with your child(ren)?

LESSONS FROM THE LITURGY

In the Mass for the Bishop Especially on the Anniversary of Ordination, the Church prays, "O God, eternal shepherd of the faithful, who tend your Church in countless ways and rule over her in love, grant, we pray, that N., your servant, whom you have set over your people, may preside in the place of Christ over the flock whose shepherd he is, and be faithful as a teacher of doctrine."[87]

• Reflect on the role of your local bishop in the life of your family. How could you foster an attitude of gratitude in your family for the work of your bishop? Consider looking for opportunities in your diocese to hear your bishop preach a homily or give a talk.

• Do you think the hierarchical structure present in the Church could help you teach your child(ren) about respect for leadership and authority? Explain.

The Seven Sacraments: Holy Orders

Mother Church has a beautiful tradition that honors the mothers of her priests. It involves a small piece of white linen, called the Maniturgium. This is the cloth that the ordaining bishop uses to consecrate the new priest's hands with sacred oil. The white linen represents the burial shroud of Christ that protected his body in the tomb. Traditionally this cloth is given to the mother of the priest because she was the first protector of this newly ordained priest in her womb. (See pages 91–93.)

• What are some important ways that you can instill an openness to a religious vocation in the heart of your child(ren)? How have you seen other mothers do this?

• Holy orders enables priests to "exercise their service for the People of God by teaching, divine worship, and pastoral governance" (CCC, 1592). Think of what you have learned from the priests you have encountered, either through their teaching, their presence at Mass, or their leadership. How could you pass along these things to your child(ren)?

The Seven Deadly Sins: Envy

• Children learn at their own pace, and all children have a different collection of strengths and weaknesses. Some mothers have it "easier" than others when it comes to teaching their children. How can we guard against being envious of other women whose load seems lighter?

• What virtue helps to guard against the temptation to envy? What are some good ways to cultivate this in our own lives, so that we can be more effective teachers of the faith?

Chapter Four • • • Mothers Accept

LESSONS FROM THE SAINTS

St. Catherine of Siena is a doctor of the Church whose fourteenth-century spiritual masterpiece *The Dialogue* records the words she heard from the Lord in prayer. "I ask you to love me with the same love with which I love you. But for me you cannot do this, for I loved you without being loved," Jesus said to her. "This is why I have put you among neighbors: so that you can do for them what you cannot do for me—that is, love them without any concern for thanks and without looking for any profit for yourself. And whatever you do for them I will consider done for me."[88]

• Consider the challenge of showing this kind of love to your child(ren). Do you ever feel that you serve your family without thanks or profit?

• Have you ever experienced emotional hurt from your child(ren)? If so, how do have responded to these circumstances? How could you consider them opportunities to love Jesus?

LESSONS FROM THE CATECHISM

"The visible church is a symbol of the Father's house toward which the People of God is journeying and where the Father 'will wipe every tear from their eyes.' Also for this reason, the Church is the house of *all* God's children, open and welcoming" (CCC, 1186). The Father's house refers to heaven, where sadness is no longer part of the picture. Here on earth, the Church's witness of open acceptance and welcome is meant to be a foretaste of this kind of bliss.

• Consider how your home shares in this heavenly experience. How do you respond when your child or husband comes home after a day at school or work? How do you encourage your child(ren) to extend this welcome to other family members?

• It can be more challenging to reconnect with those we have not seen for a while. When a grown son or daughter comes back for a visit, how do you make them feel at home?

• What kind of reception do you give to visitors, be they friends or strangers? How can you use these opportunities to teach your child(ren)?

Lessons from the Liturgy

The Mass for a wedding anniversary makes this prayer after Communion: "Open wide in joy and love, O Lord, the hearts of these your servants, who have been refreshed with food and drink from on high, that their home may be a place of decency and peace and welcome everyone with love."[89]

• Consider how the presence of joy and love in our hearts leads to a home of decency, peace, and welcome. What do you think the Church means when she refers to a home as a place of "decency"? How does our culture support or discourage this value?

• What can you do to foster decency in your home? Is your home a place of peace? If so, how do you maintain this? If not, how could nurturing joy and love help improve the situation?

The Seven Sacraments: Matrimony

Mother Church encourages us to remember our blessings even as we lay down our burdens. So we come to Mass to praise God for our families, our marriages, and our children's lives, for the joys they bring and the gifts they offer to us and to the world. How beautiful that God invites us to make a "sacrifice of praise." (See pages 43–50.)

• In the sacrament of matrimony, a man and woman promise to accept one another for life. They promise their commitment for richer or poorer, in good times and in bad, in sickness and in health. This unwavering acceptance is the foundation of the family. How can you live out these commitments in your relationship with your child(ren)?

• Can you remember a time when upholding this commitment felt like a "sacrifice of praise" to the Lord?

THE SEVEN DEADLY SINS: LUST

• At the root of the sin of lust is the objectification of another person, leading us to use someone for our own pleasure. Even outside the sexual arena, sometimes we may be tempted to think of our children in objectifying terms: Does their presence bring me pleasure or pain? How can we be sure to avoid thinking of our child(ren) as objects that are supposed to please us?

• How does practicing authentic charity or love combat the vice of lust?

Chapter Five • • • Mothers Sacrifice

LESSONS FROM THE SAINTS

Three hours before she passed away, Chiara Corbella Petrillo's husband, Enrico, asked her a question. Thinking of Christ's words, "My yoke is easy, and my burden is light" (Matthew 11:30), he said to his suffering wife, "Chiara, is this yoke, this cross, really sweet, as Jesus said?" Chiara answered, "Yes, Enrico, it is very sweet."[90]

• Consider your attitude in the face of adversity. Do you suffer with sweetness or with bitterness? How much does a mother's attitude affect the way her family experiences adversity?

• What do you think Jesus meant in saying that his burden was light? How can you help your child(ren), when they suffer, to feel this grace?

LESSONS FROM THE CATECHISM

"All his members must strive to resemble [Christ], 'until Christ be formed' in them. 'For this reason we…are taken up into the mysteries of his life…associated with his sufferings as the body with its head, suffering with him, that with him we may be glorified'" (CCC, 793). Instead of attempting to escape suffering or to pretend it doesn't exist, we are called to realistically acknowledge suffering, and then, by God's grace, to transform it into something valuable. We believe that God became man and suffered, and that we can unite our sufferings to his, making our trials into "redemptive" suffering.

- What are the situations that most test your patience? How could you approach these circumstances differently in the light of redemptive suffering?
- Can you think of a time when suffering made you stronger? Have you witnessed this in anyone you know? Explain.

LESSONS FROM THE LITURGY

The Masses of All Saints, of patron saints, and on solemnities and feasts of saints, offer these words of prayer to God the Father: "For you are praised in the company of your saints and, in crowning their merits, you crown your own gifts."[91]

The Church recognizes that the lives of the saints ultimately give glory to God. When we celebrate the merits of their holy lives, we are actually honoring God's "own gifts." Anything meritorious we do is only possible because God gave us our abilities and his grace in the first place.

- Consider the gifts God has given you and how you may be called to use them. Make an inventory of these gifts: talents, skills, sensitivities, even educational or experiential opportunities that have equipped you for certain tasks. Then, consider how you can share these gifts in your family, at your job, in your parish, or in your local community.
- What gifts have you recognized in your child(ren)? How, as a mother, have you sacrificed in order to encourage them to cultivate these gifts?

THE SEVEN SACRAMENTS: THE EUCHARIST

Each one of us helps Mother Church to make her sacrifice. We jointly offer our praise, our sufferings, our prayers, and our work together as a community of faith. And through the sacramental mystery, these little offerings of ours are joined to the one supreme offering of Jesus: his death on the cross. The *Catechism* teaches,

"The sacrifice of Christ and the sacrifice of the Eucharist are *one single sacrifice*" (CCC, 1367). (See pages ___.)

• Jesus offered up his Body and Blood for us on the cross. Regularly celebrating the Eucharist unites us to this ultimate sacrifice and keeps us ever mindful of what Christ did for us. How have you communicated the importance of this to your child(ren) through your own sacrificial giving?

• As mothers we offer our bodies and shed our blood for our children, in a variety of ways. Could recalling this fact during Mass help you feel "connected" to the sacrifice of the Eucharist? Explain.

THE SEVEN DEADLY SINS: GLUTTONY

• Gluttony isn't just about eating too much. It's about wanting more and more pleasure, to the point of saturation. Is there an area of your own life where you have been challenged to live with greater simplicity and detachment?

• The spirit of gluttony stands in direct contrast to a spirit of sacrifice. There is no room for voluntary suffering through fasting, for example, when gluttony has its way. How can we overcome our "thirst" for pleasure and comfort in order to accept suffering with a generous heart?

Chapter Six • • • Mothers Heal

LESSONS FROM THE SAINTS

St. John Bosco tells us, "In all the miracles of healing performed by Our Divine Savior, we must admire the remarkable goodness which caused Him to heal first the sickness of the soul, then that of the body. He teaches us the great lesson that we must first purify our consciences before turning to God for help in our earthly needs."[92] Because we are entrusted with the physical care of our children, we can sometimes lose sight of the importance of their spiritual care.

• Reflect on how you can help care for your child(ren)'s souls. What signs or "symptoms" can you look for to indicate that something is off balance in your child's soul? How can you be more attuned to his or her spiritual state?

• How can you help to set things right in the lives of your older child(ren) as (a) young adult(s) while still respecting your son or daughter's freedom?

LESSONS FROM THE CATECHISM

"Illness and suffering have always been among the gravest problems confronted in human life. In illness, man experiences his powerlessness, his limitations, and his finitude. Every illness can make us glimpse death. Illness can lead to anguish, self-absorption, sometimes even despair and revolt against God. It can also make a person more mature, helping him discern in his life what is not essential so that he can turn toward that which is. Very often illness provokes a search for God and a return to him" (CCC, 1500–1501).

• Consider the role of sickness in your vocation as a mother. What is your attitude about dealing with the illness of your loved ones? How can you improve your response to sickness in yourself or others?

• How has your own illness or suffering helped you be a better mother, better able to heal the sufferings of others? Do you tend toward anguish and self-absorption or toward a deeper search for God?

LESSONS FROM THE LITURGY

On the Friday of the fourth week of Lent, the Church prays, "O God, who have prepared fitting helps for us in our weakness, grant, we pray, that we may receive their healing effects with joy and reflect them in a holy way of life."[93]

• Reflect upon the various "helps" that God gives us through the Church. How many forms of spiritual assistance can you name that come from Mother Church?

• How often do you thank God for these benefits? How can you encourage your child(ren) to appreciate them?

THE SEVEN SACRAMENTS: RECONCILIATION

Jesus understood that sinners were in need of a kind of healing, just like a sick person is in need of a doctor. And he understood that he came to earth to call sinners to himself, to call them to repentance, reconciliation, and restoration. He often issued this "call" in conjunction with physical healings. And as the *Catechism* teaches, through the sacraments, "Christ continues to 'touch' us in order to heal us" (CCC, 1504).

This healing is what Mother Church offers to her children. Specifically, through the sacraments of healing—reconciliation (also called the sacrament of penance or confession) and anointing of the sick—the Church helps to comfort us in our afflictions of soul and body." (See pages 72–78.)

• Through the sacrament of reconciliation, penitents are "reconciled with the Church which they have wounded by their sins" (CCC, 1422). How have you experienced the reality that "reconciliation with the Church is inseparable from reconciliation with God" (CCC, 1445)?

• Why is it important for you as a mother to be in right relationship with Mother Church?

THE SEVEN DEADLY SINS: ANGER

• As mothers, we exercise authority and influence over our children. But when their free will contradicts our direction, we may struggle with frustrated outbursts or completely losing our temper. Far from healing our sons and daughters, this can cause emotional wounds. How can we help our children heal from such wounds?

• What are some antidotes to the poison of anger in our own hearts?

Chapter Seven • • • Mothers Celebrate

LESSONS FROM THE SAINTS

St. Thérèse of Lisieux, who lost her mother when she was only four years old, nonetheless remembered her. Perhaps because of the loss, she was all the more keenly aware of how precious a mother truly is. Thus, Thérèse once said, "The loveliest masterpiece of the heart of God is the heart of a mother."[94] The external decorations and celebrations that we prepare for our families bring an element of loveliness to the lives of our loved ones. But our hearts should be beautiful, too, and full of joy.

• Reflect on the idea of your heart being a masterpiece. What do you believe are the qualities that are most beautiful about a mother's heart?

• Consider whether your family celebrations tap into this beauty. Are these occasions heartfelt, or do they feel like burdensome obligations to you? How can you make sure parties and festive occasions are a genuine reflection of your internal joy?

LESSONS FROM THE CATECHISM
"Sunday, the 'Lord's Day,' is the principal day for the celebration of the Eucharist because it is the day of the Resurrection. It is the pre-eminent day of the liturgical assembly, the day of the Christian family, and the day of joy and rest from work. Sunday is 'the foundation and kernel of the whole liturgical year'" (CCC, 1193).

• Consider the fact that the Church insists that we have a community celebration every week! Does Sunday Mass feel like a celebration in your family? Why or why not? If you struggle with taking your family to Mass, how can you refocus on the joy that is supposed to come with this weekly event?

• Think of three specific ways that Sunday could be respected as the Lord's Day in your home. How can you make sure that the day is marked by "joy and rest from work"?

LESSONS FROM THE LITURGY
The blessing of mothers on Mother's Day from the *Catholic Book of Blessings* goes as follows: "Loving God, as a mother gives life and nourishment to her children, so you watch over your Church.

Bless these women, that they may be strengthened as Christian mothers. Let the example of their faith and love shine forth. Grant that we, their sons and daughters, may honor them always with a spirit of profound respect."[95]

• Reflect on your own mother's example. How was your mother an example of faith and love to your family? If she struggled with these things, what can you learn from the situation?

• Do you always honor your mother with "profound respect"? Why is this important? What example do your give to your child(ren) in the way you treat your mother?

THE SEVEN SACRAMENTS: CONFIRMATION

Originally, a holiday was a *holy* day. The Church established these holy days—often called feast days—and the people celebrated accordingly. In our day and age, religious value is often separated from holidays even when their origins are ecclesiastical; Christmas and Easter are cases in point. But it's important to remember that Mother Church wants her children to celebrate! She has established an entire cycle of celebrations, in fact, which we call the liturgical year. (See pages 85–90.)

• Many celebrations are embellished by giving gifts. The celebration of confirmation bestows the gifts of the Holy Spirit: wisdom, understanding, counsel, fortitude, knowledge, piety, and fear of the Lord. What impressions do you have from your own confirmation celebration? Do you still have any tokens from that day?

• Which of these gifts of the Holy Spirit do you think are most beneficial for you as a mother? Why?

THE SEVEN DEADLY SINS: GREED

• Decorating or celebrating can be tainted by greed if we fall prey to the desire to amass all the right "stuff." Buying the perfect decorations for our house or the best accessories for our parties can become a problem when we fail to be satisfied with what we have and constantly race to keep up with the latest trends. Can you devise a practical strategy for counteracting greed in the midst of decorating and celebrating?

• Can you think of some examples of mothers you have known who embody joyful celebration wherever they go? What are some of the traits or qualities they possess that helps them do this and that you would like to imitate in your own life?

Chapter Eight • • • Mary, for Mothers

LESSONS FROM THE SAINTS

In the early eighteenth century, St. Louis De Montfort wrote his spiritual classic, *True Devotion to Mary*. In this book he explains why Mary is such a help to us and encourages all Christians to make a consecration to Jesus through Mary. He writes, "Let us boldly implore the aid and intercession of Mary, our Mother. She is good, she is tender, she has nothing in her austere and forbidding, nothing too sublime and too brilliant."[96] Who would not love to have a mother such as this?

• Reflect on these qualities in yourself. Would your child(ren) be able to describe you as tender? If so, why? If not, why not?

• Do you ever come across as "austere and forbidding"? If so, how could you work to soften that perception? How could Mary help you to develop as a mother?

LESSONS FROM THE CATECHISM

"Jesus is Mary's only son, but her spiritual motherhood extends to all men whom indeed he came to save" (CCC, 501). Mary was both a physical mother and a spiritual mother. She demonstrates that a woman's vocation need not be narrow or restrictive, but can contain within it a broad mission that goes beyond her own domestic sphere.

• Reflect upon the mission that God may be revealing in your life. How might you be called to reach out as a spiritual mother to others?

- If you currently work or serve outside of your home, how can you approach these duties with the heart of a mother?

LESSONS FROM THE LITURGY

On January 1, the Solemnity of Mary, the Holy Mother of God, we pray after Communion, "We rejoice to proclaim the blessed ever-Virgin Mary Mother of your Son and Mother of the Church."[97] This feast day that christens the start of every year is dedicated specifically to the maternity of Mary. Just as each new life begins with a mother, so too the Church encourages us to begin each new year by turning to our Blessed Mother and praising God for her presence in our lives.

- Consider the fact that we are called to rejoice because Mary is the Mother of the Church. Do you have such an attitude, or do you feel disinterested or overwhelmed by devotion to the Blessed Mother?

- How can Mary's presence in your life bring you joy and happiness? In what ways could entrusting your motherhood to her protection every New Year assist you?

REFLECTING ON THE ROSARY: THE JOYFUL MYSTERIES

The five joyful mysteries of the rosary are all deeply maternal:

At the annunciation, Mary first accepts the invitation to motherhood from the angel Gabriel.

During the visitation, she shares the joy of her pregnancy with her cousin Elizabeth, who is also expecting.

The nativity is the moment when Mary gives birth and meets her child face-to-face.

At the presentation at the Temple, she entrusts her infant to God as she listens with wonder to the prophetic words of Simeon and Anna.

And when she and Joseph finally find their pre-teen son in the Temple, Jesus tells his mother, "I must be in my Father's house" (Luke 2:49).

- How do each of these five mysteries affect you as a mother? What can you learn from them?
- Do you often pray the rosary? How can pondering all its mysteries—joyful, sorrowful, luminous, and glorious—help you to imitate Mother Church in your own life?

Notes

Introduction

1. Pope Francis, "Address of Pope Francis to Participants in a Seminar Organized by the Pontifical Council for the Laity on the Occasion of the 25th Anniversary of 'Mulieris Dignitatem,'" October 12, 2013, https://w2.vatican.va/content/francesco/en/speeches/2013/october/documents/papa-francesco_20131012_seminario-xxv-mulieris-dignitatem.html.
2. Pope John Paul II, *Mulieris Dignitatem* (Boston: St. Paul Books and Media, 1998), 104.
3. Pope Francis, General Audience, September 11, 2013, https://w2.vatican.va/content/francesco/en/audiences/2013/documents/papa-francesco_20130911_udienza-generale.html.
4. *Mulieris Dignitatem*, 74.

Chapter One: Mothers Create

5. *Mulieris Dignitatem*, 65.
6. *Mulieris Dignitatem*, 64–65.
7. Pope John XXIII, *Mater et Magistra*, 1.
8. Henri de Lubac, *The Motherhood of the Church* (San Francisco: Ignatius, 1982), 39.
9. Augustine of Hippo, quoted in de Lubac, *The Motherhood of the Church*, 41.
10. Pope John Paul II, *Mulieris Dignitatem*, 77.
11. See Wayne Shealy, "The Church as Bride and Mother: Two Neglected Theological Metaphors," *Journal of Discipleship and Family Ministry* 2.2 (2012): 4–32.
12. See Joseph C. Plumpe, "Ecclesia Mater," *Transactions and Proceedings of the American Philological Association* 70 (1939): 538.
13. Cyprian of Carthage, *On the Unity of the Church*, quoted in Plumpe, "Ecclesia Mater," 540.
14. Carl E. Braaten, *Mother Church: Ecclesiology and Ecumenism* (Minneapolis: Augsburg Fortress, 1998), 2.
15. Matthias Scheeben, quoted in de Lubac, *Motherhood of the Church*, 39.
16. Cardinal John Henry Newman, quoted in *Bishop Fabian Bruskewitz: A Shepherd Speaks* (San Francisco: Ignatius, 1997), 66.

17. Pope Francis, General Audience, September 11, 2013.
18. See *Catechism of the Catholic Church* (New York: Image, 1995), 1226.
19. See *Catechism of the Catholic Church*, 1213.
20. Edith Stein, quoted in Freda Mary Oben, "Edith Stein: Holiness in the Twentieth Century," available at Dominican Province of St. Albert website, http://opcentral.org/resources/2015/01/12/freda-mary-oben-edith-stein-holiness-in-the-twentieth-century/.
21. Bennet Kelley, CP, *The New Saint Joseph Catechism* (New York: Catholic Book, 1964), 113.

Chapter Two: Mothers Care
22. Pope John Paul II, *Fidei Depositum* in *Catechism of the Catholic Church*, p. 1.
23. Pope Paul VI, "Decree Concerning the Pastoral Office of Bishops in the Church" *(Christus Dominus)*, 9.
24. Pontifical Council for the Laity, "The Pontifical Council for the Laity: A Dicastery of the Roman Curia at the Service of the Laity," http://www.laici.va/content/laici/en/profilo.html.
25. Gian Lorenzo Bernini, quoted in Norman Davies, *Europe: A History* (Oxford, UK: Oxford University Press, 1996), 569.
26. Gian Lorenzo Bernini, quoted in "St. Peter's Square," Vatican City State, http://www.vaticanstate.va/content/vaticanstate/en/monumenti/basilica-di-s-pietro/la-piazza.html.
27. Pope John Paul II, "Homily at Mass for the Families at Onitsha, Nigeria," February 13, 1982, https://w2.vatican.va/content/john-paul-ii/en/homilies/1982/documents/hf_jp-ii_hom_19820213_onitsha-nigeria.html.

Chapter Three: Mothers Teach
28. Pope Francis, *Evangelii Gaudium*, 139.
29. Madeleine Sophie Barat, quoted in Ann Ball, *Modern Saints: Their Lives and Faces*, Book Two (Rockford: Tan, 1990), 97.
30. Bishop Fabian Bruskewitz, *Bishop Fabian Bruskewitz*, 67.
31. See *Catechism of the Catholic Church*, 76.
32. See *Catechism of the Catholic Church*, 85.

Chapter Four: Mothers Accept
33. *Mulieris Dignitatem*, 101.
34. Pope John XXIII, "Opening Address to the Council," October 11, 1962, https://www.catholicculture.org/culture/library/view.cfm?RecNum=3233.

35. Pope Francis, *Misericordiae Vultus*, 9.

36. *Misericordiae Vultus*, 9.

37. Pope Francis, General Audience, September 10, 2014, https://w2.vatican.va/content/francesco/en/audiences/2014/documents/papa-francesco_20140910_udienza-generale.html.

38. *Misericordiae Vultus*, 10.

39. *Misericordiae Vultus*, 12.

40. Pope Francis, General Audience, September 10, 2014.

41. Pope Francis, General Audience, September 10, 2014.

42. *Misericordiae Vultus*, 12.

Chapter Five: Mothers Sacrifice

43. *The Roman Missal*, trans. International Commission on English in the Liturgy Corporation (Vatican City State: Libreria Editrice Vaticana, 2008), 308.

44. *Roman Missal*, 308.

45. See *Catechism of the Catholic Church*, 1368.

46. *Roman Missal*, 1063.

47. Tertullian, *Apologeticum*, The Tertullian Project, http://www.tertullian.org/works/apologeticum.htm.

48. Perpetua, "The Martyrdom of Perpetua," in *In Her Words: Women's Writings in the History of Christian Thought*, ed. Amy Oden (Nashville: Abingdon, 1994), 34.

49. Perpetua, "The Martyrdom of Perpetua," 34.

50. John Pontifex, John Newton, and Clare Creegan, *Persecuted and Forgotten? A Report on Christians Oppressed for Their Faith 2013-2015 Executive Summary* (Sutton, UK: Aid to the Church in Need, 2015), 11.

51. *Misericordiae Vultus*, 22.

52. Ball, *Modern Saints*, 400.

53. See *Lumen Gentium*, in *Vatican Council II: The Conciliar and Postconciliar Documents*, ed. Austin Flannery, OP (Northport, NY: Costello, 1975), chaps. 2, 5.

54. Pope Francis, General Audience, September 11, 2013.

55. Isaac Jogues, quoted in Francis Talbot, SJ, *Saint Among Savages: The Life of St. Isaac Jogues* (San Francisco: Ignatius, 2002), 58.

Chapter Six: Mothers Heal

56. Jerome W. Yates, Bruce J. Chalmer, Paul St. James, Mark Follansbee, and F. Patrick McKegney, "Religion in Patients with Advanced

Cancer," *Medical and Pediatric Oncology* 9, no. 2 (1981): 121.
57. Congregation for Divine Worship, Rite for Reconciliation of Individual Penitents, 45.
58. Caryll Houselander, *The Reed of God: A New Edition of a Spiritual Classic* (Notre Dame, IN: Ave Maria, 2006), 39.

Chapter Seven: Mothers Celebrate
59. "Liturgical Year," United States Conference of Catholic Bishops, http://www.usccb.org/prayer-and-worship/liturgical-year/.
60. See *Catechism of the Catholic Church*, 1655–1658.
61. "Laetare Sunday," Catholic Encyclopedia, http://www.newadvent.org/cathen/08737c.htm.
62. "Mothering Sunday," Ampleforth Abbey, http://www.abbey.ampleforth.org.uk/our-news/mothering-sunday.

Chapter Eight: Mary, for Mothers
63. *Mulieris Dignitatem*, 61.
64. Dante Alighieri, quoted in Michael O'Carroll, CSSp, *Theotokos: A Theological Encyclopedia of the Blessed Virgin Mary* (Eugene, OR: Wipf and Stock, 1982), 115.
65. *Lumen Gentium*, in Flannery, *Vatican Council II*, 420.
66. Pope John Paul II, General Audience, November 29, 1995, https://www.ewtn.com/library/MARY/JP2BVM70.HTM.
67. Pope Benedict XVI, *Deus Caritas Est* (December 25, 2005), 41.
68. *Deus Caritas Est*, 42.
69. "The Marian Devotion of St. Anthony of Padua," *Herald of the Immaculate,* http://www.ewtn.com/library/MARY/ANTHMARY.htm.
70. According to the *Code of Canon Law*, 992, "an indulgence is a remission before God of the temporal punishment due to sins whose guilt has already been forgiven, which the faithful Christian who is duly disposed gains under certain prescribed conditions through the action of the Church which, as the minister of redemption, dispenses and applies with authority the treasury of the satisfactions of Christ and the saints." To gain an indulgence, in addition to a special spiritual action, such as visiting the icon in this case, the faithful must be in a state of grace, have the interior disposition of complete detachment from sin, have sacramentally confessed their sins, receive the Holy Eucharist, and pray for the intentions of the Holy Father.
71. *Misericordiae Vultus*, 22.

72. "Prayer to Our Mother of Perpetual Help," Catholic Online, http://www.catholic.org/prayers/prayer.php?p=322.

73. *Understanding Mary Undoer of Knots* (Steubenville, OH: Steubenville, 2013), 10.

74. Quoted in "Star of the Sea (*Stella Maris*) Feast Day, September 27," *Catholic Maritime News*, vol. 79 (Summer 2015): 10.

75. Bernard of Clairvaux, quoted in J.C. Tierney, "What Is the Origin of Mary's Title: 'Star of the Sea'?" (Dayton, OH: The Marian Library/ International Marian Research Institute, October 26, 2010), http://campus.udayton.edu/mary/questions/yq/yq17.html.

76. Pope John Paul II, General Audience, September 17, 1997, https://www.ewtn.com/library/papaldoc/jp2bvm63.htm.

77. Pope Francis, General Audience, September 11, 2013.

78. *Lumen Gentium,* in Flannery, *Vatican Council II*, 420–421; emphasis added.

79. Pope Benedict XVI, "Homily on the Solemnity of Mary Mother of God," January 1, 2012, http://w2.vatican.va/content/benedict-xvi/en/homilies/2012/documents/hf_ben-xvi_hom_20120101_world-day-peace.html.

80. Pope Paul VI, quoted in *Catechism of the Catholic Church*, 975.

81. Mother Teresa, *One Heart Full of Love*, ed. José Luis González-Balado (Ann Arbor, MI: Servant, 1988), 20–24, 29, 64.

Study Guide

82. Augustine of Hippo, "Homily 1 on First Epistle of John," http://www.newadvent.org/fathers/170201.htm.

83. *Roman Missal*, 1179.

84. Teresa of Avila, *Interior Castle*, trans. E. Allison Peers (New York: Doubleday, 1989), 233.

85. *Roman Missal*, 1000.

86. Pope John XXIII, *Mater et Magistra*, 1.

87. *Roman Missal*, 1245.

88. Catherine of Siena, *The Dialogue*, trans. Suzanne Noffke, OP (New York: Paulist, 1980), 121.

89. *Roman Missal*, 1259.

90. Simone Troisi and Cristiana Paccini, *Chiara Corbella Petrillo: A Witness to Joy,* trans. Charlotte J. Fasi (Manchester, UK: Sophia Institute, 2015), 152.

91. *Roman Missal*, 598.

92. John Bosco, quoted in Kenneth Allen, "St. John Bosco," *Fr. Kenneth Allen: Ad Maiorem Dei Gloriam* (blog), January 31, 2011, http://www.fatherallen.net/2011/01/31/st-john-bosco/.

93. *Roman Missal*, 254.

94. Thérèse of Lisieux, quoted in "The Heart of a Mother," *Society of the Little Flower* (blog), May 10, 2015, http://blog.littleflower.org/st-therese-daily-devotional/heart-mother/.

95. "Blessings of Mothers on Mother's Day," 1728, in International Commission on English in the Liturgy Corporation, *Book of Blessings* (Collegeville, MN: Liturgical, 2008), available at https://www.catholicculture.org/culture/liturgicalyear/prayers/view.cfm?id=737.

96. Louis De Montfort, *True Devotion to Mary*, trans. Frederick Faber (Rockford, IL: Tan, 1941), 52–53.

97. *Roman Missal*, 183.

ABOUT THE AUTHOR

Gina Loehr is a popular author, an inspirational speaker, a theologian, and the mother of six. In 2013 Gina was chosen as one of one hundred women from around the world to be a delegate for the Pontifical Council for the Laity's study seminar on women in the Church. A frequent guest on national Catholic radio programs on EWTN, Relevant Radio, and Ave Maria Radio, Gina's other books include *Choosing Beauty: A 30-Day Spiritual Makeover for Women* and *Real Women, Real Saints: Friends for Your Spiritual Journey.*